HERBERT
HOWELLS

"I have composed out of sheer love of trying to make nice sounds":
Herbert Howells at the Kingsway Hall, London for the recording sessions
for *Hymnus Paradisi* in 1970

HERBERT HOWELLS

PAUL SPICER

Series Editor
John Powell Ward

seren

To the affectionate memory of Herbert Howells,
a lifelong inspiration; and for his daughter Ursula,
who bears her role as a 'piece of the true cross'
with patience and generosity.

seren is the book imprint of
Poetry Wales Press Ltd
Wyndham Street, Bridgend, Wales

ISBN 1-85411-232-5
1-85411-233-3 pbk

A CIP record for this title is available from the British Library

Cover: 'Dr Herbert Howells' by Leonard Boden
By kind permission of the Royal College of Music

The publisher acknowledges the financial support of the
Arts Council of Wales

Printed in Palatino by WBC Book Manufacturers, Bridgend

Contents

List of Illustrations

ONE
Lydney to Gloucester (1892-1909)

Herbert Howells was a great musician, a complex man, a devoted and devastated father, a loyal but weak and unfaithful husband, a sensualist though not a hedonist, a teacher, adjudicator, examiner, writer and speaker, and almost last of all, a composer. And yet it is because he was a composer that we most celebrate him. Why does this creative act so endlessly fascinate people? What is it about composers which marks them out as *extra*ordinary, so that we imbue them with a kind of sanctity which makes it difficult to imagine that they were actual flesh and blood? The contemporary composers we know and mix with pay their mortgages, have overdrafts, cars and electricity bills just like the rest of us. It is difficult to translate the lives of Bach or Mozart into such ordinariness, and yet of course, we know they were so.

Death is a transfiguration. In dying, composers, like writers and artists, leave a key to their souls, through which they live on, furthering the notion of immortality. Unlike most people, they leave part of themselves with us to be rediscovered with each new performance. Somehow, because of the nature of music, the composer speaks more fundamentally for all of us than any other creative artist. He articulates what we are unable to say for ourselves, and each of us hears in the composer's voice what we want to hear, at any given moment and in our own way.

Yet, for this to happen across generations, the composer articulating the message must be imbued with some sort of 'inspiration', a privileged go-between on either side of Bunyan's river flowing between life and death. Gerald Finzi said: "to shake hands with a good friend over the centuries is a pleasant thing" so recognising that the communicating power of music is a life force even when the creator has 'passed over'. Why, then, should we wish to "shake hands" with Herbert Howells in particular, in the coming pages? How does his music speak so strongly to those of us in tune with his idiosyncratic language? Why should we turn over the minutiae of his life, and paint a picture of a flawed if irresistible man, when his magical aural world already so powerfully conjures up images and emotions as strong as those of far greater composers whom it is more respectable to lionise?

The real answer can only lie in that highly personal area of emotional and intellectual response to given stimuli. Beauty, as the old adage goes, is in the eye (or in this case the ear) of the beholder. The beauty in Howells, as we will discover, lies in his inheritance; one which in great measure, he has himself bequeathed to subsequent generations.

Herbert Howells was born in Lydney, Gloucestershire on 17 October 1892. To visit the High Street in that town in the late 1990s is to see a place struggling with its identity. Ghastly shop fronts and all the usual late twentieth-century accretions vie with characterful small local businesses to deprive the place of its indigenous personality in a way which, were Herbert Howells to visit it now, would sadden his heart and force comparisons in his mind with the years he spent there as a boy. Arthur Mee's book on Gloucestershire in his series *The King's England* first appeared in 1938 and was the first genuine attempt to catalogue all England's heritage since the Domesday Book. In its 1947 edition we find the following: "One long switchback is the road between the Severn estuary and the Forest of Dean, and those who know this lovely setting by repute may be allowed some disappointment in finding Lydney, with its fame from Roman England, a small industrial town, a happy enough place to work in with fine parks to play in, but little to show the traveller" (p.289). Thus, even before the age of corporate logos and commercial premises which have further spoiled the face of the town, Lydney was in some of its aspects one of Gloucestershire's poorer offerings. But in Mee's very next breath we find something poetic in the scene; "It is a curious mixture of wooded country, growing town, factory, and a little harbour where the boats steam off with coal from the Forest of Dean. Here, when the wind blows up the wide-cliffed estuary, rippling its water into waves, we might almost fancy ourselves by the sea; we may even see a wheat-laden ship from Vancouver calling at Sharpness opposite, the farthest inland port in England" (p.290). It is with this flight of fancy that we might at last make some connection between our young composer, his impoverished family, his yearnings for beauty, and his surroundings.

For someone interested in Howells's origins the Lydney trail is both sad and fascinating. The proudest thing about the house where Herbert was born is the plaque engraved in gold on black slate which proclaims the fact. The house itself is an almost derelict shop, next door to the elegant Baptist chapel where Herbert's father Oliver would play the organ on Sundays, and from which Herbert could not escape fast enough into the welcoming arms of the Anglican church down the road. In a broadcast on BBC Radio 3 at the time of his seventy-fifth birthday Howells said "My father was a very humble businessman for six days of seven, and a dreadful organist for the seventh day" (BBC/Prizeman). It puts his poor father firmly in his place!

Herbert's bedroom, shared with his elder brother Leslie, was at the back of the house on the first floor in what is obviously an extension; part brick, and part the stone of which the main house is constructed. The only feature of note is a rather elegant small Victorian fireplace. The house is not small and upstairs there are five rooms (no bathroom, of course), but there were eight children born to Oliver and Elizabeth Howells and quarters would still have been very cramped. Given the subsequent downfall of the Howells family through bankruptcy, it is neither inappropriate nor without a certain poignancy that one sees Howells's birthplace in such a state of disrepair.

Herbert's grandparents on his father's side were James Howells of Llanelli and Laura Hutchings who was apparently of Scots origin and was known as "the flower of the forest" (of Dean). A beauty she must indeed have been, and maybe it was as much from her as anyone that Herbert inherited his startling good looks. They had five children: Mary, Oliver, Benjamin, Alfred and Howard. Oliver, the second born (1854), married Elizabeth Burgham (b. 1856) and they in turn had eight children: Florence, Leonard, Winifred, Howard, Frederick, Richard, Leslie and Herbert. The eldest, Florrie, was born in 1875 and the youngest, Herbert, in 1892.

Oliver Howells, the composer's father, was born in Littledean, a few miles from Lydney on 3 July 1854. His family all hailed from the Forest of Dean area for generations back, and the importance of this to Howells's makeup and personality cannot be underestimated. Returning to the lilting, descriptive prose of Arthur Mee again we hear that Littledean "lies amid splendid scenery on the edge of the Forest of Dean, with a favourite viewpoint overlooking the Severn valley, and an ancient earthwork called Camp Hill. Here and there the paving-stones of Roman roads peep through the grass, and Roman soldiers camped where are now the grounds of Dean Hall, a sixteenth-century house screened by trees" (p.278).

In another guide on Gloucestershire (*The Little Guide* 1914) the author, J. Charles Cox describes the Forest of Dean as "comprised of about 25,000 acres between the Severn and the Wye. It was well known to the Romans, and the great piles of refuse iron mark their extensive workings on various sites and their insufficient methods of smelting. It was reserved as a tract suitable for royal hunting in the days of the Saxon kings. William the Conqueror, as a great huntsman, made a speedy acquaintance with this district, for it was here, when he was hunting, that news was brought to him, in the spring of 1069, of the serious rising that had broken out in Northumbria. The late Norman kings extended the forest boundaries... Henry I granted the tithes of the venison of Dean to the abbey of Gloucester, whilst Henry II granted to the abbey of Flaxley not only the tithe of the chestnuts, but the right to two forges, one stationary and one itinerant..." (p.6). The history of the Forest of Dean is inextricably linked to the social and political fabric of the history of England.

Peter Hodgson, in his thesis on Howells, points out that "ethnic assimilation has proceeded slowly in some parts of the United Kingdom. Strong local and regional differences of custom, culture and dialect – even of language, *viz.* the Welsh and Gaelic – exist still among the nearly sixty million inhabitants of the British Isles. The Forest of Dean, whose occupants are regarded locally as something of a race apart and quite distinct from the people of the surrounding communities, furnishes one such instance of an ethnic enclave" (PH pp.2-3).

Whilst Howells never referred to himself as a 'forester', he was insistent that he was English and from Gloucestershire however much mixed English and Welsh blood may, in reality, have coursed through his veins. His daughter, the actress Ursula Howells, relates an amusing anecdote referring to an occasion when Howells was asked to adjudicate at an Eisteddfod when he was about thirty years old. Being short in stature and always very young-looking, someone was overheard to say in a loud voice "it's a child!" which upset him. But things went further downhill when someone else said to him later on "of course, you're Welsh" which he vehemently denied. "But you have a Welsh name" came the riposte, to which Howells replied "Christ was born in a stable but it didn't make him a horse!" (UH/PS).

The strength of his feelings about the Welsh have probably no more significance than his feeling of belonging ethnically to the English side of the border. His daughter said that he felt the Welsh to be a most unmusical nation despite the popular notion to the contrary, a sweeping statement with no basis in fact. A deeper reason can be found by examining his roots. Words like 'tribal' do not sit easily with our modern perception of civilisation. For the late nineteenth century, though, before travel became everyone's birthright and when villages and communities were more or less inbred, 'tribal' must describe pretty accurately the spirit or sense of belonging of any small rural community as it acted out its daily, monthly and annual rituals. As already pointed out, the Forest of Dean was, even then, regarded as something of a 'place apart', and to a young man profoundly aware of people and place, this distinct sense of his roots will have been strong indeed.

Much has been written about Howells's Celtic provenance, and some have questioned the emphasis laid on it particularly by Palmer in his *Herbert Howells: A Celebration*. Why is it so significant in terms of Howells's artistic personality? In their book *Celtic Christian Spirituality* (1995) Oliver Davies and Fiona Bowie assert the following as characteristic of the Celts: "The cult of a particular deity was generally linked to a specific location, whether this was a river or lake or one of the dark forest groves that so shocked the Romans. The gods of classical peoples were more mobile and their temples might appear anywhere within the Empire. We see among the Celts an interpenetration of religion and landscape in a way which surpasses anything we might find in the late classical world" (p.6).

They also draw attention to the fact that "Religion demanded sacrifice, particularly in times of war particularly when victory was paid for by dedicating the spoils of victory to the relevant god. Indeed, much Celtic wealth seems to have found its way for cultic reasons into the earth, rivers or lakes" (p.6). Is it any wonder that Helen Waddell's matchless translation of Prudentius "Take him, earth, for cherishing" found such a special resonance with Howells? But that is not all; Davies and Bowie also state that "The Celtic designer delighted in riddles and ambiguity, in rhythm and fluidity of form, and in abstract harmonies at the expense of naturalism and idealism of the Greeks. But Celtic art also showed its vigour in the ability of the craftsmen to absorb and transform foreign influences at different stages of history, whether from Greece or Rome, Etruria or Scythia, while maintaining a distinctively Celtic continuity of form and style" (p.5).

The dual significance of this in relation to Herbert Howells as a Celt is, first, the importance of place and its (originally) religious relationship with the people; and second, the artistic characteristic which is experimental, allowing foreign influence, but at the same time defining the race and giving it identity. By Howells's own admission "people and places have been a dual influence" (Argo). Who in the recent history of music has written more for specific people and places than Howells? Though a quintessentially English composer, he culled his language from a rich variety of sources; and the remarks of Davies and Bowie first cited, that the Celts "delighted in riddles and ambiguity, in rhythm and fluidity of form, and in abstract harmonies" might have been written about Howells's music itself. Asked about Howells's stylistic influences more generally, Sir David Willcocks responded that the French school was very evident besides obvious indebtedness to Elgar and Vaughan Williams. Christopher Palmer also pointed to a Dutch music critic, Alex van Amerongen, who on hearing a broadcast of Howells's *St Paul's Service* but not knowing the music, wrote to David Willcocks: "I would like to have details about the beautiful work for choir and organ you performed and broadcast on May 10 (1972). I put on the radio while it was going on, so I did not hear the announcement, and afterwards the speaker did not mention the name of the composer. I think it must have been a French composer, like Duruflé, or Litaize or Langlais. Please let me know which composition this was" (CPC p.211). Here, then, is the Celtic sensibility as Davies and Bowie have defined it; the combination of "absorbing foreign influences while maintaining a distinctly Celtic continuity of form and style". Here, too, is the defining of the race and giving it identity. As for the "delighting in riddles and ambiguity" we have only to refer to Sir David Willcocks again, who, in a broadcast and referring to Howells's *Missa Sabrinensis* said "I always assume when a composer writes something that he wants it to be heard. But in some instances it's very difficult with the music of Herbert Howells in that so much is going on at the same time. This is particularly true of his big choral and instrumental works. Sometimes I feel that he's rather like the medieval craftsman who takes enormous pains to fashion in stone some angel right up in the triforium of a cathedral where it will never be seen but he did it just for the love of it. Sometimes I feel Herbert Howells lavishes his love in his music by having some felicitous little counterpoint in some inner part which may never be heard but he knows it's there" (BBC/Prizeman).

Finally, Howells's diary for 1 March 1919 says: "I have long, ponderous thoughts on problems of musical form... hours spent in an easy chair fire-gazing, form-thinking. Most of it focused on the Clarinet Quintet. We want new experiments in form, and a sympathetic consideration of them when they are made." The 'fluidity of form' is evident at least in intention, and the picture of the classic Celt as defined in this instance is complete.

The romance of the Celtic disposition is, these days, a considerable additional colour to the character of a composer, and is also a substantial peg for our imaginations to grasp. Marion Scott, a friend to several composers of Howells's generation, and a devotee of Howells's music, put it at its clearest and most fanciful. She wrote that:

> he came naturally into an inheritance of beauty. Hill, sky, cloud, river – all these things are Gloucestershire, and behind them one glimpses the succession of centuries flowing down from the mists of time in an almost unruffled and ever-widening intellectual tide. Many races mingled their strains in the making of England. And there seems reason to believe the Romans left here a deeper mark, one less obliterated by subsequent events than in most places elsewhere. Does any sign remain today of that Second Legion, proudly named Augustan (Royal), which occupied Gloucester for so long and watched the Marches of Wales? Who knows? It is a strange coincidence that two learned authorities on ethnography – quite unknown to eachother – and on two separate occasions – singled out Howells and his brothers as perfect types of Italian Celts.
>
> (Introduction: 'Herbert Howells', *The Music Bulletin* VI May 1924, p140).

We must return to practical matters. As has been indicated, the house in the High Street in Lydney was cramped for such a large family, especially when it also served as the shop for Herbert's father's business. It was therefore not surprising that, before long, a move had to be considered, and although Oliver was only a general painter/decorator/plumber and builder, they managed to move down the hill to Regent Street to a house rather grandly called Bath Villa. These Victorian terraced houses are still there to be seen, and the Howells family home is on the corner of Regent Street and Bath Place. It is a tall, three-storey building which extends some distance down Bath Place, and the family must have warmly welcomed the additional space which the new house gave them.

Oliver was a marvellous father by all accounts, but he was not a good business man. Herbert adored his father: he was a wide-ranging and intelligent person, concerned to educate his youngest son equally widely. This included nurturing an obvious talent for music, and developing the art of observation. Thus he would rouse the boy in the early hours of the morning "to talk about stars, planets and distances" (PH p.5). Besides this Oliver was passionate about art, and was extremely well read. Whilst not being an accomplished musician he had a great appreciation of music, and this was what he encouraged in Herbert from the start. This included visiting the great churches of the region to hear the organ being played, and according to Ursula Howells, Oliver would take the young boy to Gloucester to hear the organ and the choir, carrying him piggy-back part of the way. No wonder "the immemorial sound of voices" (as he later called it) entered his blood. Another regular pilgrimage when Howells was about eight was to the great church of St Mary Redcliffe in Bristol. This early exposure to great architecture, and the place of music within it, awoke in Herbert what was much later to become his principal creative force.

His first piano teacher was his sister Florence (Florrie). As the basis for her tuition she used *Hamilton's Instruction Book*. From this volume Howells's favourites were 'The Bluebells of Scotland', and a more substantial piece gravely entitled 'For all eternity'. Florence had another pupil named Marion Pritchard who, being a few months older than Herbert, was a little more advanced than him. Once he had discovered this he was so disconcerted that he decided to abandon lessons altogether, and with them any desire to become a musician. He was nine years old. Not until 1905, about three years later, did he revoke his decision.

This hiccup in the learning process did not prevent Howells from helping out his father on the organ at the Baptist Chapel. Indeed, on one notable occasion "he caused a stir, stopping in the middle of a hymn and shouting to the congregation: 'You don't know how to sing; you must follow me!' After the service a certain Miss Stevens, who was quite a lady of the town, approached Herbert, armed with lorgnettes, and to his astonishment, presented him with a crown piece and an injunction for him to repeat his ingenious act if necessary!" (RS/RCM)

When he was eleven Herbert had had enough of the "slovenly singing" of the Baptist church and asked if he could join the parish church choir. It says much for his father's liberal attitudes that he went at once to see the vicar, the Rev. John C.E. Besant, who immediately protested: "but Bertie isn't saved!". Thus it was that "Bertie's saving" became the priority of that week, and by the following Sunday he was baptised and singing in the church choir.

Lydney parish church is a large building with a distinguished seventeenth-century spire and thirteenth-century nave. At this time it boasted a choir run by a worthy but sadly incompetent village organist. Howells later described the situation: "I assisted the tin-plate worker who was the nominal organist (wholly inadequate as such, but a loveable man – Joseph Baxter by name). The vicar found constant and clever reasons for Baxter to sing tenor in the choir while 'Howells could play the organ for us.' This became a formula!" (PH p.5)

Musical and artistic talent was unevenly distributed through the Howells family, with both his elder sisters being musical. Herbert described his other sister, Winnie, as "an accomplished musician". Leonard, his elder brother, was an artist; Howard was an amateur violinist; Frederick, who became a headmaster, seems to have missed out on any direct involvement with music as do Richard and Leslie who were both scientists, although Herbert describes Richard as being "innately musical".

An article in the *Christian Science Monitor* (June 1919) claims that "Music was always so much a part of himself that he cannot be said to have begun it at any particular date, and his early years were a kaleidoscope of piano, organ, composition, football, books, school-work, natural beauty, and again music as the medium through which everything was viewed" (CSM 14.6.19). This underlines the relative ordinariness of Herbert's childhood except in that one area of his overriding interest – obviously something extremely unusual in someone of his background.

After two years at the local Dame's School (1896-8) he went on to Lydney's Church of England Elementary School (1889-1905) and from there won a scholarship to attend the local grammar school. It was here that his developing musicianship gave him a special place in the school's life and began to earn for him a reputation which brought him to the attention of the local great and good. Such people were soon to give him the opportunity he so much needed to receive tuition at an altogether higher level than Lydney could offer. At his grammar school Herbert was put in charge of music for morning prayers and for providing the music for theatrical performances, composing and adapting music as necessary.

Through his efforts both at school and church the young Howells's reputation was spreading fast, and he was brought to the attention of the local Squire, Charles Bathurst (later first Viscount Bledisloe of Lydney and Governor General of New Zealand), by his headmaster who suggested that he needed more expert tuition than was available locally. The Bathursts realised the plight of the Howells family in its poverty and Mary Bathurst (the Squire's sister) undertook to pay the three and a half guineas which Dr Herbert Brewer, the organist at Gloucester Cathedral, charged for the series of ten lessons per term. So, from 1905, aged thirteen, Howells travelled once a week on a Saturday morning from Lydney to Gloucester for a piano lesson. This was taken in the music room which Brewer had recently built on to the organist's house (7 Millers Green) to the left of the front door. Howells called these lessons 'perfunctory' and he found them rather disappointing. Brewer's method being: "This Saturday: the 1st Sonata by Mozart; next Saturday the 2nd Sonata by Mozart, and so on" (RS/RCM). Herbert later came to respect Brewer as an organist.

Mary Bathurst would not go on paying Howells's tuition fees indefinitely, and so the burden was thrown back on his father who simply could not afford it. "Brewer was 'somewhat niggardly', and was not prepared to allow any delay in the payment of his fee and sent his pupil home with an ultimatum to this effect" (ibid). It was then another year and a half until Charles Bathurst intervened on Howells's behalf, persuading Brewer to take the boy on, now aged sixteen, as an Articled Pupil.

Howells could smell freedom in the streets of Gloucester and a life which could offer considerably more than the limited resources of his native Lydney. Gloucester, after all, was one of the three homes of the Three Choirs Festival, which at that time was the pre-eminent music festival in the country, and by far the oldest in existence. Thus all the major singers, orchestras and composers of the day would converge on whichever of the three cities of Gloucester, Hereford and Worcester was hosting the meeting that year. Once a year in September they would go through the ritual of performing the most popular choral works of the day, spiced up with gradually increasing numbers of new works for the critics to lampoon and the public to tolerate impatiently whilst awaiting a performance of the work they had really come to hear – usually *Messiah, Elijah* or *Gerontius.*

The audiences attending the performances of these great choral works in those days were extraordinary. In his book *Three Choirs: A History of the Festival* Anthony Boden tells us that the audience at Worcester Cathedral for a performance of *Gerontius* in 1905 numbered 3,053 people. That is a vast assembly for such a building. Heavens knows what some of these people will have heard, stuck in all nooks and crannies!

Howells apparently did not attend any of these Three Choirs meetings until that at Gloucester in 1907, and thus is unlikely to have met Ivor Gurney yet, though they later became the closest friends. Gurney, a year older than Howells, was singled out in 1904 as a leading chorister at Gloucester Cathedral when the soprano Madame Sobrino failed to turn up in time to sing second soprano in the 'Lift thine eyes' trio in *Elijah*. Gurney stood in, to great acclaim. According to his mother Ivor was "frightened at his success when he got home he hid in the kitchen everybody saying Ivor Gurney had been singing with Madame Albani" (ibid p.147).

Whatever the reality of his contacts at Gloucester at this early stage, Howells cannot but have been aware of the two leading local musical figures, Edward Elgar and Hubert Parry. Both were, of course, featured in that 1905 Festival. In his wildest dreams Howells can hardly have imagined how important they were both to become to him personally, and how he would come to revere one of them, Hubert Parry, almost above all others throughout his long life.

TWO
Gloucester towards London (1909-1912)

At the time when Howells was studying at Gloucester with Brewer, cathedrals worked a valuable apprenticeship system for their up-and-coming musicians which has long since disappeared. The modern 'organ scholar' is very much a poor relation, and tends only to be a cheap way of acquiring an extra assistant organist without any of the academic associations of the 'articled pupil' as Brewer would have known it. It was a highly practical solution to the daily needs of the cathedral's music-making, whilst also providing a thorough musical education for those selected. The Articled Pupil was given a thorough grounding in musical theory, harmony and counterpoint. He was also given organ tuition and was trained in the art of accompanying the Cathedral's services.

When Howells became one of Brewer's Articled Pupils in 1909 he joined two others, Ivor Gurney and Ivor Novello; an unlikely pair! Howells recalled them later in life: "poor Ivor [Novello] could never do his strict harmony and counterpoint. He used to get me to do it on the QT, as they say, which I did. And finally he departed to London and the fleshpots. There was a much greater man, although not more loveable, Ivor Gurney, who I think you would put amongst the six greatest songwriters this nation has ever produced. And he and I used to go for walks which lasted for three days and nights" (BBC/Prizeman). Howells recalled another occasion when, sitting at the organ console in Gloucester Cathedral, he saw the great east window built to light the great Perpendicular heights of the choir and filled with glass celebrating the victory at the battle of

Crécy in 1346 ablaze with light. Seeing this as a "pillar of fire in my imagination", he said to himself "God, I must go to Framilode!" He walked out and was away for three whole days (MH p.21).

Apparently, these occasions took place without the knowledge or permission of either of the boys' parents who were either worried sick, were extremely trusting, or knew all along, making this a rather romanticised version of events. When Howells and Gurney were together on these walks, talk would be about music and English literature, a love they both shared passionately. Above all, they shared a deep and abiding love of the Gloucestershire country-side which was by far the most powerful influence on them both. As Howells went on to say: "I used to sit with Ivor Gurney on a hill half way between Gloucester and Cheltenham and from there, on a clear April day (shall we say), when the visibility was second to none, you could see the whole outline of the Malvern hills thirty miles north of that hill. Gurney said to me one day 'look at that outline', he meant the outline of the Malverns, he said, 'unless that influences you for the whole of your life in tune-making, it is failing in one of its chief essentials'. And of course outlines of hills, and things, are tremendously important especially if you are born in Gloucester-shire, God bless it" (BBC/Prizeman).

That "hill halfway between Gloucester and Cheltenham" was 'Chosen' Hill at Churchdown, which became such an important icon to both Howells and Gurney – and other composers of the period – and which features prominently at significant moments throughout Howells's life. Howells's and Gurney's walks are some-thing they shared with other English composers of the period, notably Holst and Vaughan Williams, who famously went on long expeditions. Is it any wonder that the countryside which featured so largely in their day-to-day existence should find such reflection in their music?

It is difficult to say when Howells began composing. He would probably have said that he had been composing all his life. There is little extant juvenilia, but manuscripts exist of one of a set of *Four Romantic Piano Pieces*, an *Arab's Song* which is dated 1908. In the following year, when he became an Articled Pupil at Gloucester, there is another composition called *Marching Song*, dated 16 January

1909, 'arr. by H.N. Howells'. His first example of song writing also dates from that same month, *My Shadow* for a poem by Robert Louis Stevenson.

These early pieces are typical of Howells's unformed style. His influences are obviously composers to whose music he was exposed regularly and who included Mendelssohn, Parry and Elgar, as well as a host of lesser composers whose music would feature on the Gloucester Cathedral music lists. He was well aware, however, of the failings of these poorer composers as he recorded in his diary for 11 January 1919: "A day in Gloucester with [Arthur] Benjamin – he marvelling at the cathedral, I at the stolid stupidity of the cattle which invade Gloucester on market days – particularly on Saturdays. Dr Brewer in the cathedral, played Bach's *Passacaglia* as an act of grace to Benjy: and then took him to drink tea in his house in Palace Yard. Poor Benjy! He listened to the childish absurdities of Clark Whitfield's evening service in E... and sure, he marvelled at them more than at the Norman pillars close by!"

Those who have written Howells off as a one-language composer who never developed stylistically should acquaint themselves with his early works. Howells's major disadvantage was to become known purely as a composer of church music. He did not begin writing church music in earnest, however, until the 1940s when he was in his fifties, and it was not until 1956, with the composition of the *Collegium Regale* settings, that he started to change the landscape of music for the Anglican church with his canon of settings of the evening canticles. Howells had certainly reached his mature style by this stage, and it is only those who have examined the scores, and heard the now extensive recordings of his earlier works, who will know just how far his style travelled before reaching the sound-world for which he became so well-known.

Already in 1909, however, Howells was well into the Gloucester scene and familiar with what it had to offer. Friendships were being forged, and a new relationship developed with Dr Brewer based on a healthy mutual respect which had developed since the days of the 'perfunctory' piano lessons. In the manner of the great pedagogues of the period, Brewer was an authoritarian teacher, and a harsh disciplinarian whom the young Howells held in awe. It was therefore with some trepidation that he approached Brewer about the programme for the next Festival: "I asked him, with great daring, because I was rather frightened of him, 'Sir, do tell me, have we got anything interesting coming down in September at the Festival' [which was at Gloucester that year, 1910]. And he said 'Oh, yes, some strange man who lives in Chelsea has been writing something to do with Thomas Tallis the great Tudor composer'. I said 'really?' but he emphasised the curiosity side of it you see as if he hadn't got much faith in this strange man in Chelsea!" (BBC/Prizeman).

The "strange man from Chelsea" was of course Ralph Vaughan Williams, and the work his *Fantasia on a Theme of Thomas Tallis*. Howells singled out its first performance as amongst the most important seminal experiences of his life. "I heard this wonderful work, I was thrilled, I didn't understand it, but I was moved deeply. I think if I had to isolate from the rest any one impression of a purely musical sort that mattered most to me in the whole of my life as a musician, it would be the hearing of that work not knowing at all what I was going to hear but knowing what I had heard I should never forget."

So said Howells many years later in a BBC broadcast (ibid). He also recalled:

Lovely first week in September came. With it came the composer from Chelsea, a magnificent figure on the rostrum, a younger but more commanding version of the then Foreign Secretary, Sir Edward Grey. He was nearly thirty-nine. I gazed at him from the sixth row of the 'stalls' in the nave. (Beside me – in a crowded audience – an empty chair). I was seeing him for the first time. But what mattered was that it was Tuesday night, an Elgar night; a dedicated Elgar audience, all devotees of the by then 'accepted' masterpiece *The Dream of Gerontius*.... But there, conducting a strange work for strings, RVW himself, a comparative (or complete?) stranger; and his *Fantasy* would be holding up the *Dream*, maybe for ten minutes? In fact, for *twice* ten, as it happened.

He left the rostrum, in the non-applauding silence of those days, thanks be! And he came to the empty chair next to mine, carrying a copy of *Gerontius*, and presently was sharing it with me, while Elgar was conducting the first hearing I ever had of the *Dream*. For a music-bewildered youth of seventeen it was an overwhelming evening, so disturbing and moving that I even asked RVW for his autograph – and got it! I have it, still.... And I still have what I now know to be a supreme commentary by one great composer upon another – the *Fantasia on a Theme of Thomas Tallis*.

(*Two Hundred and Fifty Years of the Three Choirs Festival* 1977)

After the performance Howells and Gurney wandered the streets of Gloucester for hours, unwilling to return home and unable to sleep from the power of the experience they had just shared.

The gestation period of Vaughan Williams's music in Howells's mind was long and deep and showed little or no evidence of immediate effect. The two works which later surfaced and can be counted as directly attributable, are the *Elegy* for viola solo, string quartet and strings (1917) and '*Master Tallis's Testament*' for organ (from *Six Pieces for Organ*, 1940) which Howells referred to as a "footnote to the Vaughan Williams' work, and even more a personal throw-back to the Tudors" (PH p.8).

What Howells was witnessing was no less than one of the defining moments in the process of the birth of the English musical renaissance. The two new influences which broke the hold of nineteenth-century German and Italian music over the entire establishment at the time were English folk-song and Tudor polyphony. All our principal composers and educators at the time were either Leipzig trained or influenced by the Germanic tradition, and the Royal Academy of Music was set up to reflect the fact.

Frank Howes, in his penetrating analysis of the roots of the English musical renaissance, isolates three men: Hubert Parry, Charles Stanford and Alexander Mackenzie, as being the visionary teachers who were responsible for rehabilitating English music, and creating the environment in which it could flourish on its own terms and not as a pale imitation of another tradition. This was done through training a new generation of composers in such a way as to lead them into developing a musical language and style which became unmistakably English. The Royal College of Music was founded in 1883 in response to the inadequacies of the Royal Academy of Music which had led "to a project for a new institution with a wider outlook, a more comprehensive curriculum and higher standards" (FH p.29). It was also a critically important time in the nation's educational life. Compulsory state education was about to come into force, and there was a growing confidence in the ability of our composers and performers. The Royal Academy refused to tow the line which the Royal College was throwing them, and it was not until Alexander Mackenzie became principal there in 1888, that the older institution began to emulate the ideals of its rival in South Kensington.

The Royal College of Music was, of course, to become the anchor point of Howells's whole career, and two of the revered names above his closest mentors. But that is was yet some way in the future. Vaughan Williams's new work, which so affected Howells that September evening in 1910, offered the impressionable youngster a fleeting vision both of his future and of his musical and spiritual roots. It gave him a clue to the identity for which, still only seventeen, he was searching, and began to unlock the door to his musical imagination. No wonder then, much later, when Howells and Vaughan Williams had become close friends, the older composer said that he felt Howells to be "the reincarnation of one of the lesser Tudor luminaries" (CPS p.11). The emphasis on this influence and the effects of the *Tallis Fantasia* on Howells were powerfully put when he said: "Ralph and I felt and reacted to things musically in a very similar way, and if some of our works are alike in any respect, it's not, I think, merely a question of influence but also of intuitive affinity. We both came from the same part of the world and loved it dearly; we were both attracted by Tudor music, plainsong and the modes – my interest in folk music was perhaps more for its modal colouring than for its human associations. We felt we needed to write in these modes and in the pentatonic scale; there was no question of our using them simply because they were novel" (CPS p.12).

Stylistically, this was still in the future, but the influences were beginning to be set at this point and the desire to compose became an overwhelming passion. Howells threw himself into the task with extraordinary vigour. In 1911 Gurney left Gloucester to go to the Royal College of Music to study composition with Sir Charles Stanford and quickly persuaded Howells to follow him. Thus it was that Howells decided to leave the security of his position at Gloucester with Brewer in order to devote himself entirely to composing. This had something to do with lack of money to maintain his position at the cathedral, but it also gave him the chance to concentrate on the writing of the portfolio of works which he had to present to the Royal College of Music for consideration for the open scholarship in composition – his passport to study with Stanford.

Howells was fired with visionary enthusiasm at the prospect of studying at the College. He was also, presumably, fired by the lure of London life, its musical and social whirl affording an almost total contrast to the village and small-town provincial city life he had known up until then.

So it was that all of a sudden the floodgates opened and the first series of truly representative and important works began to flow from his pen. His Opus 1 was an *Organ Sonata in c minor* which was dedicated to Brewer's assistant at the cathedral, Ambrose Porter (later organist of Lichfield Cathedral). The manuscript of this work is missing and the work only survives by the accident of a Howells devotee and Brewer pupil, Tustin Baker, having copied it out and had it bound. Baker was organist at Sheffield Cathedral and the copy was handed on after his death by his widow first to Hubert Stafford, sub-organist at the cathedral, and then to Graham Matthews who became organist there in 1967. It was quickly recognised as the 'missing' early Sonata and edited by Robin Wells and Graham Matthews for publication in 1991.

In that edition they assert, on the evidence of Tustin Baker's copy, that it is Howells's opus 2. However, in Howells's diary for 1919 (the first year he kept a diary), he lists his main works to date with their opus numbers, and the *Organ Sonata* is clearly listed as Opus 1. This is hardly a serious issue, however, as Howells abandoned the use of opus numbers altogether in about 1930, and there are other works given opus numbers at the time which do not feature at all in the 1919 list.

The work is fascinating and provides many clues to the way Howells's musical language developed. His principal influence at this stage seems to have been Elgar. There are many hints in the sonata form first movement at passages from *The Dream of Gerontius*;

evidence, too, that he knew Elgar's *Organ Sonata* and Parry's organ music. There is also much evidence of a gift (or perhaps a penchant?) for improvisation, although at this stage, as amply demonstrated in the slow movement, it seems rather limited in its scope. On this evidence it consists mainly of circular ramblings in sixths and thirds, sometimes with that other favourite organists' device, the dominant pedal point. All of which sound pleasant enough in Gloucester's generous acoustic but are not very convincing in this context. The early part of this movement is reminiscent, too, of one of Karg-Elert's lack-lustre offerings. If anywhere in Howells's early output, this movement seems to underline a problem which dogged him to a greater or lesser degree all his life. He was not a natural tunesmith, and he could too easily resort to note-spinning with the best of them to get him round a 'block' in inspiration. This does not imply that he *couldn't* write a tune, just that in the normal process of writing he would naturally compose contrapuntally even at this early stage. When that was no longer appropriate, or he wanted a change in texture or idea, the muse could easily desert him and he would find himself 'improvising' himself out of his corner and thus weakening his argument. Bar 40 to the end of the slow movement is a good example of this.

The third movement is stronger and has an interesting idea in presenting a linking slow section at the start of the movement before he begins a highly assured fugue. There is an almost tangible sense of relief when he gets to the set-piece fugue and a demonstration of the kind of technical know-how which marked him out right from the start as one of the leading musical minds of his generation.

Gerald Finzi, writing a wide-ranging appreciation of Howells in the *Musical Times* in April 1954, made a veiled reference to Howells's weaknesses when comparing him with Vaughan Williams. Finzi said:

> Although Howells belongs to a generation of English composers which received its formative impact from native sources rather than from Leipzig or Paris, nothing could be more remote from the slow, oak-like growth of the older composer, with his hard-won and entirely personal technique, than the diamond-cut brilliance with which Howells seems to have been born, and

which, on a technical level, has never failed him. It would, in fact, be far more reasonable to think of the consummate ease of Mendelssohn when considering Howells's particular dexterity.
  (MT 4.54 p.181)

Some readers may feel that this criticism is unduly harsh in what is, after all, a juvenile work written when Howells was still only nineteen years old. These comments are not intended as criticism, but as an observation and a pointer to a fault-line in his creative spark. It will become increasingly significant as the story develops and will help to explain considerable anomalies which arise as he grows to maturity.

There is one moment in this *Sonata* which points at future developments and which stands out like a beacon of light amid the late-Victoriana of the rest of the work. It is eleven bars from the end of the whole work and is a false-relation where a B natural in the left hand is contradicted by a pair of B flats in the right hand. This is completely out of character with the work as a whole (not that other, more innocent, false-relations, do not occur) and seems to wave a tiny flag of rebellion amidst the general conformity. This says clearly that Vaughan Williams's message delivered so powerfully on 10 September the previous year had been heard loud and clear, and that the clearing system in Howells's young brain was trying to sort out the conflicting messages it had been receiving. A chink of light shines brightly and points, however indistinctly as yet, at the fertile ground where the deepest and richest seeds have been sown almost unwittingly; and to what effect!

With the composition of his opus 2, a *Cycle of Five Songs* for low voice we reach a significant moment in Howells's life on two levels. First, he gives us his first song-cycle written quickly between 30 August and 21 September; and second, they are written for Dorothy Dawe, a mezzo-soprano who, nine years later, was to become his wife. Looking first at the music; it is obvious that Howells wrote these songs in a white heat of inspiration. Single days are written onto the title page as the date of composition of each song. Whilst two of them, *The Twilight People* and *The Waves of Breffany* stand slightly apart from the others (30 August and 14 September), the remaining three were composed on three successive days (19, 20 and

21 September). The songs show Howells in a different light from the *Organ Sonata* and represent a significant advance on the achievements of that work. It is almost as if he has been liberated by being able to take his music out of church. Undoubtedly, the source of his inspiration was the beautiful young woman with whom he fervently hoped to form an attachment. The fact that he was already engaged to another girl (Kathleen Smale, of whom more later), does not seem to have deterred him from starting to woo Dorothy Dawe, the new object of his attentions, by sending his songs post-haste to her. She responded: "I will make another attempt to thank you for your *Cycle of Songs*. There is one thing I would like to tell you if I may and that is – you have forgotten in composing that you were *not* writing for one as clever as yourself.... However, I will do my best, in my spare minutes" (CPC p.14). She goes on to say that she will not have anyone to play them for her until she can "have the pleasure of getting the composer to do so" (ibid). She also makes clear that she will return them in time for Howells to send them to London for submission for his scholarship examination at the Royal College.

The songs give a further fascinating insight into Howells's motivation and influences at this early stage. Elgar leaps from the page again and again and, like the *Organ Sonata*, whole progressions are 'lifted' from *Gerontius*. The moment, for instance, in *The Devotee* (to a poem by Thomas Keohler) when the poet says "How strange that nature too should know the ecstacy [sic] of sin's wild glow", the music takes on the same three-part texture and the thirds/sixths meanderings which Elgar gives the orchestra to accompany Ariel close to the start of Part 2 of *Gerontius*, and the voice begins with that same falling semitone figure which is a feature of that section. The instruction *Nobilamente*, one of Elgar's most characteristic markings, also appears at the end of that same song. In the fourth song *The Sorrow of Love* to a poem by Seumas O'Sullivan Howells recreates the wonderful moment in *Gerontius* where Elgar, close to the start of the work, sets Gerontius to sing "Tis this strange innermost abandonment" to the accompaniment of a widely-spaced and richly-scored first inversion G major chord. In Howells's song it is in E flat, and the effect is if anything even richer. The phrase returns three times.

The overriding mood of the whole set of songs is one of sadness and, to some extent pathos, and there is little or no relief from this general mood. But then pathos was, by his own admission, "a quality which has moved me more than any other in music – even since boyhood". He cites three works which were particularly influential in his own upbringing; the Vaughan Williams *Tallis Fantasia* already discussed; Delius's *Sea Drift* and Brahms's *Third Symphony*. "Parts of *Sea Drift*", he said, "are (for me) the saddest I've ever heard. The Brahms' coda (last movement) is not quite the same thing, but it is (like Vaughan Williams's ending to his *Fifth Symphony*) a sort of benediction upon the work as a whole" (PH p.8).

There are some extraordinary things in Howells's early song cycle, and at the points where they occur the effect is of a caged song-bird desperate for release. It is clear that sheer quality of sound, rich, perhaps thick textures and harmonic colour are going to preoccupy Howells as he develops from this early stage to the point where he has command of his own voice.

In the meantime, released from his duties at Gloucester Cathedral, he became organist of Aylburton church at the princely salary of £4.10.0 a year. Aylburton is a village very close to Lydney, and he would easily have been able to walk from home to the church on Sundays to play for the services. The organ in the church is a little one-manual instrument with seven stops which is very sweet-toned, and would have pleased him in its quality of sound, if not in the versatility of its specification.

It is difficult to pinpoint just when the family business "went to smash" (CPC p.11) as Howells put it, but it certainly happened in his early youth. His father was far too kind a man whom everybody loved, and he bankrupted himself by not insisting that people for whom he worked should pay their debts promptly. According to Ursula Howells, people used to come to him and say: "I can't afford to pay you", and he would say: "don't worry", and he just let them get away with it. He had absolutely no head for business and he suddenly woke up one morning to discover the worst (UH/PS).

In a small town in the early years of the century bankruptcy was a serious issue and there was a terrible sense of disgrace about it. The family, while not being cold-shouldered by their closest friends, were ostracised by the community. Howells said of it: "My father was a very humble businessman... and ultimately trying to run a business which he didn't understand he became bankrupt. And you would have no idea of the cruelty of small-town people. After that, the people who had been calling themselves friends of his would cut him dead in the streets. If I was invited to a party, when supper was served, I was sent into the kitchen or into the butler's pantry" (BBC/Prizeman).

The effect of this on an impressionable and sensitive adolescent can only be guessed at. The young Herbert was caught up in it at the worst possible age. Being a rather pretty boy and the youngest of the family he was sent down to the butcher at closing time to ask for leftover scraps for the family to eat. It was pathetic and degrading and Herbert never forgot the experience which lay close to the surface throughout his life. It affected his approach to money, but far worse it sowed the destructive seeds of self-doubt which took some years to take hold, but which when it did, as we will see, drained his confidence in what he was writing.

As a postscript to this episode Howells had good reason to be grateful to Lord Bledisloe, or "Bloody Slow" as he was known locally. Not only had the family provided funds for his tuition in Gloucester, but after the bankruptcy when Herbert was asked to go to a function at Lydney Park (the Bledisloe home), and was taken straight to the kitchen by the servant, Bledisloe discovered what had happened and promptly took all the other children to the kitchen as well. In our more enlightened times this may seem a patronising act, but in those days it would have been a lifeline to Herbert, and a signal from the squire as to how he should be treated by others.

THREE
South Kensington towards Salisbury
1912-1917

"I knew nothing of Stanford until Ivor Gurney fired me, in 1911, with the idea that one's only salvation lay in South Kensington. For there, Gurney alleged, was a man teaching composition at a place called the Royal College of Music. A further year of scriptorial struggle elapsed before I laid my life-and-death efforts on the great man's table" (PH p.10).

Those 'life-and-death efforts'; the *Organ Sonata*; the *Five Songs for low voice*; a *Sonata for violin and piano* (now lost) and a set of piano pieces called *Summer Idyls* (sic) which were discussed in the last chapter were submitted for scrutiny at the Royal College of Music early in 1912. Howells was examined by Parry, C. Harford Lloyd (who preceded Brewer as organist of Gloucester Cathedral) and Stanford. He won the much-coveted scholarship and began his studies at the College on 6 May 1912. His teachers were the Director, Sir Hubert Parry, for music history and literature, Sir Charles Stanford for composition, Charles Wood for harmony and counterpoint, Sir Walter Parratt for organ, and Sir Walford Davies for choral techniques. This was quite a formidable team, and one which was to exert a huge influence over him.

Despite the fact that Gurney was at the College, and Herbert therefore had at least one person in London whom he knew, the experience must have been extremely daunting. He was a genuinely country boy, probably still extremely gauche despite having some of his rougher edges rubbed off at Gloucester, and still with serious social hang-ups about his family situation. He simply relied on the brilliance of his natural musical talent to carry him through. As it turned out he could not have attended anywhere better from all these points of view. When asked what College life was like in those days, he replied "like a cosy family".

Whilst at College he was with a hugely talented intake of students (not all in his year) which included Arthur Bliss, Arthur Benjamin, Eugene Goossens (in fact all the Goossens family were there), Frederick Thurston the great clarinettist, and, of course, Gurney. Word quickly spread of Howells's brilliance, and much later on, this topic came up when talking to Arthur Bliss in a radio broadcast. Bliss recollected their first meeting:

"The first time I think I ever met you was in 1913 and you had already been at the College for a whole year and were considerably more advanced than I was who had already taken a degree in music at Cambridge fooling away most of the time as one does when life is thought of with a capital L. I came to the College and I saw for the first time that here was someone who was much more gifted than myself. I never forgot that...."

[Howells responded:] "I remember you coming to me with a copy of *Crime and Punishment* by Dostoevski, and I pretended that I had not even heard of Dostoevski... and I got the idea that you fellers – my fellow students – if I may call you that, had got the idea that I was on a perch and that perhaps I ought to come off it."

[Bliss replied:] "I think you were put on the perch... I think I followed you generally in lessons the same day with Stanford and I heard nothing except Howells for a long time, and I mean I realised, of course, when I saw those works that you had written with this impeccable handwriting as though you had written them off easily the day before and so on, and they were played and everything, I said to myself, you know, what is the use of going on struggling like this. I remember that perfectly well. You were a most disheartening person!"

(BBC 1972)

Howells had, in fact, fallen firmly on his feet and had landed an almost perfect set of teachers for his needs. Principal among these were Stanford, the loveable Irishman with the notorious temper which Howells never experienced; Wood, another Irishman, whom

Howells described as "the most completely equipped teacher in my experience"; and Parry, of whom Howells later said "Hubert Parry? I could talk for ten years about Hubert Parry!" Parry was indeed one of the most remarkable men of the moment; an aristocrat, a visionary, a politician, a considerable composer sometimes touching genius, and a remarkable and innovative educator. He was also, most importantly in Howells's eyes, a Gloucestershire man, who owned an estate just outside Gloucester at Highnam. All these men, and many others, instinctively felt that Howells was the leading musician of his generation, and that all aspects of his education should be nurtured with care. They also knew that he had to be de-provincialised and given not only the technical ammunition to take on the musical world, but also the personal armour required when a creative artist is thrust at an early age into the limelight. In this, had they lived long enough to see it, they would have been in some respects disappointed.

At the start of his time in London Howells was very homesick. He was so poor that he was unable to afford the train journey to Lydney, and he would sometimes go and buy a platform ticket at Paddington Station just to watch the trains leaving for Gloucester. He missed his family, the countryside, the fresh air and his walking. The London streets were no substitute for that. There were other compensations, however, notably the hum and the buzz of the capital city, the exciting musical life, and the performances of new works. There were also the ever-present friendships forged within the 'cosy family' of the College – notably with Gurney, Benjamin and Bliss – and a widening net of influential people with whom he regularly came into contact and who took him in and liked to be seen with the new 'bright young thing' on the musical scene. This was especially and significantly so of the women with whom he became friendly.

Howells had taken the Associateship examination of the Royal College of Organists in 1912 just before taking up his scholarship at the RCM and had passed. The RCO had taken over the highly decorated building next to the Royal Albert Hall which had originally housed the RCM. Later it outgrew the premises and moved to the purpose-built building in Prince Consort Road in 1894. His ARCO was the first of a string of qualifications and prizes which were to mark his inexorable progress over the next few years.

In these softer-edged, politically correct days in which we live at the end of the century it is perhaps difficult to imagine how strict a regime was maintained in educational establishments. Not that the students of the day did not try to pull every possible string to make their lives easier than their teachers would have it. But in that, things seldom change. Howells's comments on Stanford as a teacher are highly illuminating:

> None of us lived in the easy atmosphere of neutrality when we took lessons with him. Mastery of subject carried with it, in him, a very definite sense of where he stood; and that definition ill accorded with vagueness of attitude in others. By methods in which long practice taught him to believe, he brought his pupils themselves to know where and for what they stood.
>
> Whatever else one might have become under his shrewd guidance, it never could have been a wobbler, a neutral, a befogged practitioner. It was often his way to make a student fight hard in defence of a point of view, an expression, or a mere chord. Failure in this was apt to bring trouble upon the pupil. But that the defence generally prevailed, and brought self-reliance – as Stanford, in his wisdom, always hoped it would – ought to be clear to anyone who observes the remarkable degree to which most of his pupils have established their own identities in composition.
>
> (PH p.12)

This was from a Stanford devotee. Bliss was rather harder in his appraisal: "The only thing that didn't stimulate me [at the RCM] I'm afraid was the teaching. I've learnt more from my contemporaries, as every artist does, than from my so-called masters" (BBC 1972). Howells's response was characteristically diplomatic:

> I know it is usual to say of Stanford that he was a great teacher. But on his own confession sometimes, he would say that there were certain pupils who defeated him. He was defeated... among others by Frank Bridge who he said was a magnificent musician, but to him the enigma of Frank Bridge's personality stifled Stanford's efforts to help him. And the other person that he reviewed in the same sort of way but in quite another sense

was Ivor Gurney, of whom he said that "that was probably potentially the most gifted man who ever came my way".
(ibid)

A good example which Howells gave of Stanford's teaching methods relates to Gurney. Howells went along with Gurney one week to sit in on his lesson. They sat either side of the great man. Gurney, whose manuscripts were completely chaotic, sat waiting impatiently for Stanford to deliver his assessment. Eventually the moment came when Stanford's gold pencil moved to make an alteration. "There, my boy! That puts it right." Gurney looked to see what had been done and said "Well, Sir Charles, I see you've jiggered the whole show." Stanford threw him out, but after closing the door remarked to Howells who was left still sitting apprehensively by the recently vacated desk "You know, I love him more each time" (MH p.35).

Wood could be equally demanding, though could not have been a more different personality from Stanford. Howells remembered him vividly:

> As teacher, Charles Wood was as gentle as any man could be in the presence of his pupils – gentle alike to the bunglers and the brilliant. He did not make extortionate demands upon us. Because he asked little some of us made it a principle never to go empty-handed to his lesson – I adopted that principle, and honoured it for three years – until the day came when I had nothing ready for the afternoon lesson. They used to say he could do a setting of the *Magnificat* at high speed. For my part, I could copy with like swiftness. On that destitute morning I copied a six-page and six-part setting of Raleigh's *Even Such is Time*. I had taken the work to him three years earlier – in my first term. My swift copying was done to preserve the principle of unbroken productivity. Blandly and without qualms I presented it. For four pages he murmured approval. On the fifth his pencil began making slow circles round one line. Then – with gaze averted – he said, 'Do you remember the trouble that bit gave us three years ago?'
> (CPC p.306)

One of Stanford's first actions was to send Howells off to the recently built Westminster Cathedral to hear R.R. Terry's choir. Terry was a remarkable musician who led the revival of Renaissance polyphony. He was the first conductor in recent times to perform the Masses of Byrd, Tye and Tallis liturgically and, as Patrick Russill has pointed out, this had the effect of "transforming national perceptions of our musical history and heritage" (Chandos p.4). He also encouraged new compositions from the principal composers of the day, but this eventually led to his parting company with the cathedral who felt that he was "too bold in his choice of works". Terry required very high standards of his choir, and so the music which was being heard as if for the first time acquired a special quality and aura for those privileged to witness it.

The effect on Howells was immediate and underlined Vaughan Williams's noted remark much later in his life of Howells's "intuitive affinity" with the Tudors. Within weeks of Howells's arrival in London and his exposure to this music he had written his *Missa Sine Nomine*, or *Mass in the Dorian Mode*. The score is marked May/June 1912 and it marked the beginning of a fruitful and reciprocal relationship with Terry and his choir. It was also his first professionally performed work.

The *Mass in the Dorian Mode* is fascinating because of the extreme purity of style. On one level it could be described as a technical exercise because Howells was obviously flexing new-found musical muscles, and yet the music itself raises it way above the level of mere academe. Howells was simply 'in tune' with this style and wrote as happily in it as in any style which he was forming of a more individual hue. The polyphonic example learned from the likes of Byrd and Tallis infused his work for the rest of his life. It is interesting that in 1903 the Vatican issued a *Motu Proprio* encouraging composers to learn from their ancient forebears in the style and restraint of their works for the church. Howells needed no such encouragement at this time, as this Mass clearly shows.

Away from the church he was beginning to look to a broader canvas than he had hitherto attempted. His close friendship with fellow student Arthur Benjamin provided the necessary stimulus for work to begin on a *Piano Concerto* which was to be his first purely orchestral work. Benjamin was an Australian from Sydney and came over on an open scholarship to study composition with Stanford in

1911, the same year as Gurney. He and Howells remained lifelong friends until Benjamin's death in 1960. He was a thoroughly engaging, outgoing sort of man with an impish sense of humour and a great affection for Herbert. Several of Howells's friends used to play on his names when addressing him in letters. Gurney used often to call him 'Howler', while Benjamin had a variety of appellations such as 'Dear L'il Erb' or 'Dear old 'Erb'. Howells was certainly small in stature, and this, as Christopher Palmer has pointed out, inspired a certain protectiveness in others. He was also extremely good-looking, dressed very well (heaven knows how he afforded it in his student days) and, as his daughter Ursula wryly noted, "was unbelievably attractive to the female sex, and was equally attracted to them".

The first *Piano Concerto* was premiered at the Queen's Hall in July 1914 with Arthur Benjamin as soloist, conducted by Stanford. Howells reported that in the days following it received its "murder by critics". He quickly withdrew the work, describing it as "unduly pompous". The score is kept at the RCM Library (along with the majority of Howells's manuscripts), but is mysteriously missing its final few pages. Did Howells remove them when he thought of revision in 1971? Were they lost? Not even the solo piano part or the orchestral parts survive, and so unless a completion can be written it is impossible to perform and record this important work. It is a tantalising mystery, and a sad loss, for the work as we have it is remarkably strong and virile, with a great sense of purpose in the manner of much of Howells's music of this period.

Not everyone 'murdered' the work in their reviews. Eaglefield Hull, for instance, felt it to be "a magnificent work, well worth ranking by those of Rachmaninov which we hear so frequently" (MO 2.20). Gurney, too, was loud in his praise of the work and in a letter from his regimental base at Seaton Delaval as late as 1918 wrote: "Why, to think of the c minor Concerto makes me tremble; it is so much above me in everything save (I believe) pure beauty" (LF p.90). But here, already, we see Howells the ultra-sensitive composer withdrawing a work on the slightest pretext because criticism was generally unfavourable. It is a trait which was to dog him all his life and is one of the principal reasons why so little of his orchestral and chamber music is known today.

Sensitivity in response to criticism fortunately did not prevent him from maintaining a steady flow of important new works in this first golden period of composition. The next major orchestral work which he completed in 1914 had the enigmatic title *The B's*. This was not what some people imagined, a homage to Bach, Beethoven and Brahms, or even Bruckner, but a light-hearted suite of five pieces dedicated to friends whose real or nicknames began with B. So there is an Overture: 'Bublum' (Herbert himself); Lament: 'Bartholomew' (Ivor Gurney); Scherzo: 'Blissy' (Sir Arthur Bliss); Mazurka: 'Bunny' (Francis Purcell Warren); and March: 'Benjee' (Arthur Benjamin). There are two important aspects to this work (apart from the marvellous music which is fresh and invigorating); one is the emphasis on people which has already been noted as an important element in Howells's make-up; and the other is that this is the first time we see Howells in quasi-miniaturist mode setting dances, or dance-type movements. These were to become absolutely central to his whole creative process and they occur repeatedly in his output.

The work was well-received at the time and Dan Godfrey, the supremo of the Bournemouth Municipal Orchestra, programmed it for the orchestra's 1919 season. The title, however, was seen as a handicap by many, and almost inevitably the work sank without trace until 1948. In that year Howells resuscitated two movements in the form of *Music for a Prince* in honour of the birth of the Prince of Wales.

Another example from this period of both difficult movement titles and a work composed largely of short dance-like movements is his 1915 *Lady Audrey's Suite* for string quartet. The rather quaint titles of the four movements are *The four sleepy golliwogs' dance; The little girl and the old shepherd; Prayer time* and *The old shepherd's tale*. Each movement is prefaced by a short poem which gives the movement its character. The most extended movement is the third which is a set of variations, one for each of the days of the week described in the poem, with its individual magic for the little girl who is its central character. It is the essential innocence of the music and its inspiration which marks it out and, at the same time, causes problems for contemporary critics. Howells noted in a diary 'round-up' of his works to date that "it has had a 'run' in America; and quite an unusual number of performances in this country".

The *Three Dances for violin and orchestra* composed the same year did not even have the limited extra shelf life of the two revived movements of *The B's*. They were composed for an extremely young, and obviously very gifted fellow student, George Whittaker (only thirteen at the time of composition), who played them at a College concert after which they, too, were abandoned to gather dust on the shelves of the RCM Library where they were discovered by the present author and first recorded for the BBC in 1989. They are a truly lovely set of pieces with a haunting central movement at their heart – a real romance, full of youthful warm-bloodedness and a quieter, more level-headed passion than was to sear through many of Howells's later works. As a postscript to this work, it is amusing to note that at the end of the first of these dances Howells notes in the score that it was finished in bed on 2 January. Youthful habits don't change over the years.

The principal feature of all the orchestral works of this early period is an extraordinary command not only of technique, which seemed never in doubt, but of the kind of sound world he wanted to inhabit. To some observers the orchestral sound Howells conjures can appear thick-textured. It is certainly true that he enjoys using his orchestra fully, but he creates his own unique orchestral palette, for example very often employing a piano. This is an idea obviously culled from Stravinsky but is used to great personal effect. The results are usually opulent and, from this early period, richly rewarding. It is surprising that none has ever caught on despite a measure of temporary success at the time in a few cases, but much of that has to do with Howells's own attitude to his music. If others did not pursue and promote his music, he never pushed it beyond its first performance. This was true of the 1915 song set simply called *Five songs for high voice and orchestra op.10*. The manuscript of these songs is missing but we do know that they were scored for strings, string quartet, flute and clarinet, an economical orchestra for the young man who enjoyed big canvases. The songs were later revived and re-scored for full orchestra, in 1928 for the Three Choirs Festival at Gloucester.

In their original version Howells set two German poems by Goethe and Theodor Storm which he had to translate "from the language of the Hun" as he put it. In the revised version the Storm song is removed and replaced by a magical setting of James Stephens's *The Goat Paths*.

The year 1915 saw Howells flexing his compositional muscles in various directions which were to be important to him. He began his first serious and characteristic organ works with the first set of *Psalm Preludes* written between 1915 and 1916. These pieces, which are still the staple diet of organists all over the world, are outstanding minia- ture tone-poems based on selected verses from the psalms. They underline a problem which reoccurs throughout his organ music, however, and that is that they are too accessible, too playable by the average organist, and therefore subject to innumerable hackings which are far removed from the inspirational improvisation from which they undoubtedly sprang. Howells became a fine improviser, and when he was acting organist of St John's College, Cambridge in the Second World War, hardly played any prepared voluntaries (as we will see in Chapter 8). How fascinating it would have been to be a member of the choir or congregation in that chapel with a tape- recorder to hand! What an insight would have been given into the way his creative mind worked.

Also from this same year came the start of another important series of organ works, the *op.17 Rhapsodies*. Looked at superficially the cynic might be tempted to ask what difference lay between the *Psalm Preludes* and this first *Rhapsody*. The essential difference is not a stylistic one, nor the fact that there is a quiet opening, a dramatic build-up and a falling away to a peaceful end. Rather, there is no programmatic element. This is absolute music, and these pieces underline a principle which governs almost all Howells's music from about 1913 when one might detect the beginning of a personal style, that of 'mood creation'. Howells, and others on his behalf, was articulate on this subject and best described it when writing about Vaughan Williams's *Pastoral Symphony*.

> He neither depicts nor describes. It is not his concern to 'make the universe his box of toys'. He builds up a great mood, insis- tent to an unusual degree, but having in itself far more variety than a merely slight acquaintance with it would suggest. In matter and manner it is intensely personal. Even its detractors (and there be many) will admit its compelling sense of unity,

though they count it death to the work. If you like, it is a frame
of mind (not consciously promoted).
(M&L 4.22)

This 'frame of mind' is perhaps Howells's most telling phrase
there, and Katherine Eggar in an article about Howells written in *The
Music Teacher* in 1923 made another key observation; namely, that "the
most English of all" Howells's qualities was that of "remoteness":

> It is that in us as a nation which must account for our amazing
> literary history – that hold upon the deep things of the mind
> which persists in our tradition, in spite of all our levity, our
> gullibleness, our commercialism, our stupidity, our superficial
> contempt for learning. Some might say that the 'remoteness' in
> Howells's music is due to his looking back to the past in music;
> others, nearer to the point, might say that the quality of the
> music to which he looks back is also 'remoteness'.
> (TMT)

The critic Edwin Evans also made many deeply perceptive points
in an article written for the *Musical Times* in 1920. Developing the
theme of Howells's mood creation, he points out that "at other times
it creeps in imperceptibly, and one realises that the atmosphere of
the music is radically different from what it was a few pages back,
without having noticed the transition" (MT 2.20). Interestingly, he,
too, refers to the "mysticism for which perhaps *remoteness* were a
better word" (ibid).

It is certainly a pertinent question as to where Howells's music
came from. Given the significance of the Gloucestershire countryside to him and the impossibility of knowing from where a creative
artist receives his 'spark', it would seem likely that an inborn talent
for musical expression found its inspiration and initial outlet in the
inspiration received from that very local countryside. Evans again
puts his finger on a strong pulse when he says that "the main characteristics are therefore a lyrical realisation of the beauties that
unfold themselves to the eye of the tone-poet amid rural surroundings, a sense of openairishness combined with a feeling for distance
that engenders a strain of mysticism, alternating with a healthy
cheeriness which has a different ring from the gaiety of cities". This

brings up the whole issue of English 'pastoralism' which has been dogged by such bad press in the second half of the twentieth century. Much of this has been enlivened by Elisabeth Lutyens's famous 'cowpat' comment. It is therefore very important to set the record straight in such a narrative as this.

All that has been said by Eggar, Evans and Howells himself above tells much of the background to the style. There are many others of course, but one further thought is relevant at this point. Lutyens wrote off the music of this period as chocolate-box prettiness, the portrayal of nymphs and shepherds in an idyllic landscape dancing to the ubiquitous 6/8 metre. It is perfectly true that there is a whole swathe of music in this vein: German's *Merry England* is a classic example. For the serious English composer, such as Howells, the countryside provided a completely different kind of inspiration. There was much more of the sense of what the psalmist sang when he wrote "I will lift up mine eyes unto the hills, from whence cometh my help" (Psalm 121), than any mere reflection of beauty in photographic terms. It is a spiritual longing and fulfilment through communion and sympathy with nature coupled with a preoccupation with innocence, and therefore loss of innocence, which are all part and parcel of the issue of nature as opposed to the corrupting influence of towns.

So much for Howells's musical style and creative impetus for the moment. Another crucially important development occurred in Howells's life at this time. He discovered that he not only enjoyed writing words but that he was also extremely good at it. Having not had any formal education beyond school, there had not been any particular reason for him to write structured and well-argued prose. At college however, he entered an essay for the Director's History Essay Prize every year between 1913 and 1916. The first of these elicited a letter from Parry which underlines the fact that he could still surprise:

> Your essay certainly needed no extenuation! I think it is a surprising performance and congratulate you on it heartily. There's such lots of independent and just and reasonable thought in it. You'll see when I come back what a high opinion I have of it.
>
> I hope you have been having a pleasant time and that your eyes are behaving themselves serviceably.
>
> (CPC p.17)

Whilst Parry's words must have been an enormous encouragement, Howells was still smarting over the lacklustre reception of his *Piano Concerto*. This probably had more to do with Stanford's conducting than the work itself. Sensitivity aside, however, Howells was attacked by something far more serious than the barbed comments of the press. He found that he was constantly exhausted, and that he was having serious problems with his eyesight. This was the onset of Graves disease which, at this stage, was undiagnosed but which was causing problems that made him think he was simply overworking. He *did* work hard, but apart from his natural desire to get on and make the most of all his opportunities, this most probably was also to purge the family debt; not in real terms since he was not earning any significant money at this stage, but in his mind. For he was earning his keep by preparing himself for the best career which he could muster. This included ensuring that he had all the best qualifications for the purpose. In July 1916 he sat and passed the daunting Fellowship examination of the Royal College of Organists together with his friend Herbert Sumsion (later organist of Gloucester Cathedral, who won the Turpin Prize).

Howells's illness, however, was extremely serious. It was a heart-related condition which meant that he found it difficult to walk and talk at the same time, he had a pulse rate of something in the region of 130, and his eyeballs protruded. It was debilitating and really took hold sometime in 1915. There is a letter from Parry to Howells dated 31 December in which Parry expresses extreme concern, but also practical help:

> I am very anxious about your eyes. How do you think it would serve if you saw Dr Bower of Gloucester? He is an eye specialist of considerable reputation, and I think his advice would be worth having. Among other things he is a very keen amateur musician and would be for that reason extra glad to help. I would gladly write to him if you liked, and would also gladly provide for any expense entailed.
> (ibid)

This mention of help with expenditure is typical of the generosity of the man, and throughout Howells's long illness and his extensive hospitalisation he never once received a bill (which he could not anyway have afforded to pay).

When Graves disease was diagnosed he was given six months to live. He was twenty-three years old, was the great hope of the rising generation of composers and was to be cut down in his prime without ever seeing a military uniform. Howells's fellow students were enlisting fast as the war machine ground itself into action. Bliss, Benjamin, Gurney, 'Bunny' Warren, all of them were snatched away to an uncertain fate to 'serve King and Country'. Howells, ironically, was prevented from joining the army because of his illness. What was supposed to have killed him in six months prevented his destruction by mine or gunfire, enabled him to be in a position where he could unwittingly help in the advancement of medical science, and gave him a longer life than any other member of his family.

Believing that he would have only a short time to live, the specialist dealing with his case asked Howells if he would be prepared to try out a new treatment as yet untried. Thus it was that Howells travelled to St Thomas's Hospital twice a week for two years for radium treatment. He was the first human being to be given it. That he lived to ninety must have been beyond everyone's wildest expectations. In fact, the doctors were working so much in the dark that they had no idea how much radium to give him. Eventually, they stopped when his neck (where the injections were given) showed signs of burning.

The process of recovery and recuperation was long and painfully slow. He spent part of each week having treatment in London, and the rest of the time in Lydney where his mother looked after him and he would have whole days in bed.

Howells could never bring himself to stop working, and letters from several teachers and friends testify to this. Parry, in his address to students at the end of Howells's final term at the RCM, said that "his wholehearted ardour has caused him many times to overtax a constitution none too robust". His friend Arthur Benjamin wrote him a 'lecturing' letter in August 1916:

> You are not strong enough. Why, oh why do you not take a complete rest in your holidays? Fool that you are. Yes, I'm angry. Herbert you must look after your valuable self. Think of Dorothy and think of the great minds in the weak bodies that have been. For you are *not* strong.... Dear boy, if you have any

friendship for me prove it by resting. I want to see you great. Miss Scott tells me that you were overworked last term.... As for the war. Do not worry that you are unable to take part in it. That's what healthy beasts like myself are for.

(CPC p.33)

Happily, in one sense, all these entreaties failed to stop Howells composing, and 1916 brought in a golden harvest which proved itself to be Howells's first truly vintage period.

Back in Gloucestershire a move of signal significance was being made by a clergyman whose life intimately touched both Howells and Gurney. Canon Alfred Cheesman began his career as a curate at All Saints, Gloucester and in 1890 he had stood as godfather to Gurney at his baptism together with the vicar of the church, as Gurney's parents had presented their child for baptism with no sponsors. Cheesman was one of the strongest influences over Gurney in his formative years and was very well known to Howells. In 1912 he moved to be vicar of Twigworth, a village a few miles from Gloucester. Twigworth was to become central to the lives of the Howells family in their time of happiness, as the place where Herbert married Dorothy Dawe; and when tragedy truck, as the place where their son Michael was to be buried so few years later.

Twigworth is within shouting distance of Churchdown, also known locally as Chosen, where the hill mentioned earlier with the wonderful views over the Malverns has acted like a magnet to artists and musicians over the years. The crown of the hill is a beautiful place where an ancient church looks solemnly but comfortably down on the valley below to the greater grandeur of Gloucester Cathedral. It is a very English form of hilltop in stark contrast to the way such places are treated on the continent. Just below the church, which is surrounded by magical yew trees, there is a small sexton's cottage which was where Gerald Finzi caught influenza from the family who lived there which was to set off his final illness and precipitate his early death in 1956. It is a place of many connections and resonances.

On their talkative walk to Chosen Hill, Howells and Gurney would arrive breathless at the top after a solid couple of miles of climbing and they would sit and excitedly discuss the beauty of the scene around and below them. Howells had an additional reason for feeling drawn to Churchdown as Dorothy Dawe, his song-bird dedicatee of the early *Five Songs* and object of his affections since 1911, lived there too. Many a diary entry extols the virtues of the lanes of Churchdown and what inspiration lay in wait at his journey's end. In the meantime, sitting one day (Saturday 12 February 1916) in his lodgings in 48 Aldridge Road Villas, London and kept waiting for twenty minutes for a meal to be served, he took a sheet of manuscript paper and wrote the first bars of a *Piano Quartet in a minor*. From these initial scribblings Howells made a proper start on the work back in Churchdown a few weeks later at 'Glengarriff', the house where Dorothy lived with her foster parents. He completed it in June (MT 2.20 p87-91). This was by far Howells's most important chamber work to date, and is still regarded as one of the most significant works by a British composer of the period. He dedicated the work to "The Hill at Chosen and Ivor Gurney who knows it".

Although Howells did not give the work a programme as such, Marion Scott, a devotee and friend of both Howells and Gurney (whom she helped enormously through the war and afterwards), was quite explicit in giving details of a 'nature' programme which helps colour the work's three movements.

> When the movement opens it is dawn, and the hill wind, pure, eternally free and uplifting, is blowing: gradually the greyness changes to colour, the half-light to full radiance, mystery to vision, dawn into day.
>
> The second movement is the Hill upon a day of midsummer, and the thoughts are those which come as a man lies on the grass on his back gazing upward into the vast vault of the sky, seeing the "giant clouds go royally", watching the blue depths of height untold flow outward to surrounding immensity until, floating on the flood of wonder, mind and soul are almost loosed from their earthly anchorage.
>
> The Finale is the Hill in the month of March, with splendid winds of spring rioting over it, and flashing in the exuberant rush, wild daffodils goldenly dancing.
>
> (TMS)

Of all Howells's early works this is the one which stakes out his territory and which marks him out as a composer of style, technique, inspiration and substance. There is much of Ravel's suave assurance in this work, and a highly impressionistic style is one of its hallmarks. Many have commented on the similarity of its panache and language with Ravel's *Piano Trio* which certainly pre-dates the work (1914) but which Howells almost certainly had not yet heard. Of more positive interest is the fact that so many of Howells's musical fingerprints first appear here. It is as if someone has unlocked a door and that the 'clearing house' in his mind referred to back in 1910 had just given him access to a hitherto restricted zone.

Stanford probably could not believe his eyes. No doubt he puffed and pouted, but whilst the famous gold pencil hovered over the odd detail, he must have been wide-eyed at the maturity and assured touch of this new offering. No wonder he later fondly referred to Howells as "his son in music", and even later bequeathed him his historic signet ring which his daughter now wears.

Given that there is so much which is French in style in the *Quartet* it is surprising that Stanford gave it such a warm endorsement. Stanford after all, so steeped in everything Germanic, was based in the wholly opposing camp and regarded the colourful harmonic language developing all around him in his pupils as "modern stinks". If one really dismantles the bricks of Howells's style, every-thing about his approach to sound and substance is much more akin to what was happening across the English Channel. First there is Debussy, and then by influence and instinct, Ravel, Lili Boulanger, Duruflé and onwards down the line via Messiaen to the outrageous hedonism of the choral music of Pierre Villette. Howells would not have liked Villette's music which he would have seen as a vulgar extreme, he himself never straying beyond given limits. It was Debussy's colour, sensuousness and evocation of mood and place; Ravel's fastidiousness, and his repressed nature almost desperate to find expression in music; Boulanger's exquisite sound world; and Duruflé's marriage of old with new which spoke most directly to him. In this last case, it is no wonder that the British have taken Duruflé's tiny output of music to their hearts in recent years; and no surprise to find, almost without exception, that devotees of Howells's music also love the music of France's arch-impressionist in church and organ music. Where Howells looked back to Tudor polyphony or to folksong-inspired melody (which he said he used more for its modal rather than human associations), Duruflé took plainsong as his inspiration. The results in the hands of either composer are remarkably similar when subjected to their impressionist treatment and to the extravagances of lavish orchestration.

The *Quartet* was the real start of Howells's celebrity. Stanford was insistent that it be submitted for consideration by the trustees of the newly founded Carnegie Trust Fund Musical Works Scheme who funded the publication of a number of major new works. Initially Howells felt that there was little point in his competing as all the major British composers of the day were submitting manuscripts. Stanford himself sent up his opera *The Travelling Companion*. In the event, Howells posted Stanford's work and Stanford insisted on doing the same for Howells's *Piano Quartet*. It was a typically generous gesture.

Howells heard the result of the competition on 7 April 1917. The Archdeacon of Sarum, Canon Carpenter, called on him before 9 a.m. to give him the good news that the *Quartet* was to be included in the first list of publications. As Howells said, "mine was the only unknown name to appear in the first list of works to be published under the auspices of the Carnegie Trust – in fact my piece was the very first to be published. There I was rubbing shoulders with names that were household words – Stanford himself, VW, Bridge, Holst, Rutland Boughton and so on – and it was largely due to this happy stroke of fortune that I became known" (BBC/Prizeman).

Amongst the many accolades which followed its various performances Vaughan Williams's of many years later in 1942 was heartfelt: "It is most beautiful – Gerald [Finzi] & others had often told me about it & said how good it was but I had fought shy of it – I don't like piano quartets usually & thought this would be the same – But I feel this is all that I should have liked to have done & have never succeeded in doing" (CPC p.434).

Vaughan Williams also made some very illuminating observations regarding Howells as a technician: "When you people who know your job do get the right sow by the ear by Jove you do get it – but somehow I believe that your very competence somehow prevents you often perceiving which the right sow is & leaves it to us bunglers to get hold of it by accident" (CPC p.434). Vaughan Williams, always original and free from any constraints of received technique, style or form, developed his own techniques which worked for his purposes. This was what Finzi was referring to when he commented on Vaughan Williams's "oak-like growth" in comparison with Howells's "diamond-cut brilliance" (MT 4.54).

Howells's brilliant student career at the Royal College was drawing to its natural conclusion and he had to think of his professional development beyond its 'cosy' walls. He obviously had to earn a living as he had no private income to support a life entirely devoted to composition, unlike Gerald Finzi who had the means to hide away in his lovely purpose-built house in Berkshire. Howells was so well regarded at College, however, that it was inevitable that he would be head-hunted for a good job. That was what happened on 12 February 1917 when he was offered the post of assistant organist at Salisbury Cathedral by Walter Alcock. He wrote to Dorothy Dawe:

> It has all been the work of one day – to-day. I met Dr Alcock at College at mid-day; he explained that he would like to have me as assistant at Salisbury; he told me that I should have rooms in the Cathedral Close (the loveliest in the land) and a salary of £100; he spoke to Sir Hubert [Parry] and Sir Walter (Parratt) at lunch-table at RCM; I had interviews thereafter with Sir Walter (at 2 o'clock) and Sir Hubert (after History Lecture) and with Sir Charles [Stanford] (at 4.30). At 4.35 I told Dr Alcock that all the professors named thought it a good thing for me; and I am going down to Salisbury to 'look round' on Thursday March 1st; and shall, if all goes well, begin there on the following Monday or Tuesday, Dr Alcock expressed delight about it: and, Dosse, I'm pleased about it too! In these days of uncertainty it is certainty!
> (CPC p.64)

In the middle of a period when Howells was being regularly hospitalised, and had not yet been released from, at the least, a life-threatening disease, it is strange that he can talk of anything as a certainty. On 22 February 1917 at 3.10 p.m. ("Truth to tell – in a train at Paddington. Bound for Gloucestershire") he wrote a letter to his friend Harold Darke, organist of St Michael's Cornhill and conductor of the St Michael's Singers. It is extremely revealing about his state of mind at the time and is worth quoting in full:

My dear friend,

Further truth to tell is that "something has cropped up" – for me. And the only dark hue in the whole affair is its primary cause. You know that Humphrey Bourne went to delightful Salisbury to be assistant. Perhaps you have not yet heard of his illness, and of his having to abandon the place and the work, and return to London. For him it is all very sad.

I am going to Salisbury! Does it surprise you? (say 'Yes!'), pain you? (say 'No'), disappoint you (say 'No' again!). Of course for all Bourne's friends there is a feeling of pity for the unlucky chap – fine fellow that he is! I am really sorry, as you must be.... And somehow or other I feel a sort of unworthiness to take up a position which he would have loved so, and of which he is robbed so soon.... Perhaps the feeling I have is more rational than logical.

I must admit the joy I feel, on the other hand at this unexpected opportunity which presents the possibility of my building up in my mind a healthier and happier set of associations than those which have played such havoc with that past of my musical state of mind which had relation to church music. I have talked to you often enough of the sort of repugnance which even some of the best church music kindled in me – merely because it all filtered through that nasty mood which has been part of my musical mentality ever since Gloucester. Work under such conditions as Salisbury will present will be so pleasant, and the companionship of a man like Dr Alcock so very different from the inhumanity of Brewer, that I soon ought to be at mental peace with church music. And indeed, dear fellow, I want *no* quarrel with the inside of our cathedrals. There is work to be in them – good, hard, sound musical work – which may lift them out of the general musical disrepute into which so many of them have fallen. I shall attempt to do my bit towards what must of necessity be a big collective but general effort if it is to be successful. You are already doing a Trojan's share towards that end, and I have always respected and loved you for it. You have 'hitched on' to life properly: you are a man with an appointed and appropriate place in the scheme of things musical. The fact that I have seemed hitherto, a more or less waif and stray member of the musical community has weighed on me more, perhaps, than even you have suspected. I look forward to Salisbury as a set of conditions which will rid me of this feeling. I shall do my utmost to be a real help to Dr Alcock, and I hope it may be in me to please him.

It was good of him to offer it to me. From its first mentioning, I felt I should like it. (I had not forgotten Oxford or St Anne's: but both these were extremely uncertain for me.) I did not accept the idea however, without first asking Dr A to speak to Sir Hubert and Sir Walter about it. They both favoured it... and Sir Charles too (he was very nice about it). I would have liked speaking to you too (for you are among the few to whom I feel I *can* speak with some advantage to myself) had you been near at the time.

I hope you think that a period at Salisbury will have its blessings for such as person as I am (let me hear from you).

I expect you know that the salary will be £100, and there are rooms in The Close for me. That should be nice. I shall come to London one day a week as long as my scholarship lasts. And I hope I shall obtain an occasional glimpse of you.

(We are just dashing through Maidenhead! Writing is well nigh impossible. But I must explain that I am going down home for a long 'weekend' (until Tuesday) in order to get together music and books which I may want to send to Salisbury. And I am worried about my dear little niece, Betty Huzzey. She is rather severely ill.)

If you are writing to Bourne, I should be so grateful if you would let him understand how I feel for him about his Salisbury disappointment, and my feelings about taking a place which he would have loved so. Will you do that?

And give my greetings to your mother.

    My love to you,
    HH

That Howells, too, was so soon to have to relinquish this cherished post through continuing ill-health is an extraordinary irony, and one which cannot have pleased the Salisbury authorities in having to search for yet another assistant organist so soon, and at such a difficult time with the war still grinding on and taking so many of the best young men.

FOUR
Salisbury to London (1919)

And so Howells arrived in the lovely surroundings of the close at Salisbury, the newest recruit to the cathedral organ loft which in those days was regarded as one of the pinnacles of musical achievement in British musical life. No wonder he was thrilled. No wonder, too, that he recognised in Salisbury's beauty a reflection of Gloucester and Gloucestershire, and saw in it also a new source of inspiration for his creativity. He must have felt that fate had indeed smiled favourably upon him despite his weak condition and his continuing treatment in London. But it cannot have been without a glance sideways at his friends being slaughtered and maimed on the battlefields of the Great War, still raging, that he indulged his pleasure. Ivor Gurney wrote from the trenches on 11 March 1917.

> Your appointment pleases me immensely, and when the letter reached me, in a crowded dugout, full of men weary of labouring in the mud, it was as light in the darkness. How well I remember that exquisite Close with the Cathedral so delicate yet so strong, soaring like a pure desire. It gave me hope also for myself that one of my friends had had good fortune – the pleasure was a little selfish, so far selfish; and I thought how I might return to College, and come down for one day to see you, full of joy at work accomplished and anxious to see yours, and *Lady Audrey's Suite*. Of course you deserve all these things, but your getting them must nevertheless be received with welcome at the start. Well done! Go on and prosper and take all the joy out of life you can.
>
> (CPC p.43)

Gurney's letter perhaps strains at the effort of good will, and who can be surprised when he was up to eyes "in the most appalling mud"? He would have been more than human if he had not felt some degree of envy towards his friend for whom, despite his illness, life seemed rich and comfortable in relation to his own. Stephen Banfield in his biography of Finzi quotes Joy Finzi quoting a letter which her husband wrote to the composer Robin Milford: "Who will ever know that so far from Gurney & Howells having been great friends – & any article by Marion Scott & even several loyal articles by Howells himself go to show this – that Gurney had the greatest contempt for Howells. J.W. Haines, who knew them well in Gloucester says that Gurney used to say "Oh, Howells will just get married, & that will be the end of him, and a Dr of music which is what he is best fitted for". Both of these tragic prophesies seem to have come true... (GF p.64).

Howells's relationship with Ivor Gurney has come under the spotlight several times in recent years in books by Michael Hurd (*The Ordeal of Ivor Gurney* 1978), Christopher Palmer (*Herbert Howells: A Centenary Celebration* 1992) and most recently Stephen Banfield (*Gerald Finzi* 1997). All seek answers to anomalies in the hitherto accepted fact that the two were bosom friends from their Gloucester days until the tragic final period of Gurney's incarceration in a mental asylum.

Banfield points to Howells's strained relations with Finzi when Howells would not accept Finzi's treatment of his mother when he was in the process of composing. However, Banfield puts this down more to the electric sensibilities of their stage of life, and some degree of professional jealousy and point-scoring, than to any real animosity. There was certainly a feeling of resentment in the air when Howells proved to be of little or no help when Howard Ferguson and Gerald and Joy Finzi were trying to sort out Gurney's song manuscripts after his death. But we run ahead of ourselves. Gurney lived (if it can be called living) until 1937, twenty years from the point we have reached in Howells's life. And yet of those twenty years, only five more were left to him before his incarceration; five years when all his mental anguish was gathering to the point when he could no longer control his own impulses and reactions, and that was well on the way by the time Howells moved to Salisbury.

Howells's plan, set out in a detailed letter to Dorothy, was to spend one day a week in London while his scholarship lasted at the College. He entertained great ambitions of moving on from Salisbury to one of the "important organistships", and felt that Dr Alcock was the perfect person to refer him upwards:

> Alcock is universally loved; he taught Gurney the organ at College; he was, until recently organist of the Chapel Royal, St James's Palace; and is still the teacher of Princess Mary. He is one of the finest organists in the kingdom, and, of course, he will be (in all probability) the next organist of Westminster Abbey. So you see, Dear, I shall be with a man who can appreciably help one.
> (CPC p.65)

As it turned out, Howells was at Salisbury for a very short time. Research carried out by Richard Seal, until recently organist at Salisbury, and quoted in an article by John Weeks in the *Musical Times* in April 1986, shows that Howells was at the cathedral from mid-February to mid-May "at the very most". Weeks goes on to state that Howells had told Richard Lloyd (organist of Hereford and then Durham Cathedrals) that "he seemed to have spent most of his time travelling between Salisbury and London for medical treatment" (MT 4.86). So much for his vain hope expressed in the letters to both Dorothy and Harold Darke of a day a week at the College. It seems odd that there is no mention of his medical condition in either letter, or of the regular visits to St Thomas's Hospital which he must have known would have to continue for the foreseeable future.

However brief his stay, he certainly made his mark at Salisbury. There is a photograph of him sitting proudly amidst the cathedral choristers, one of whom was a "dear little boy called Stewart ('Ooce!' we call him...). He is a loveable child: 8 years old; very keen on music, and very able with it. I am composing six little pieces for him to perform (he called them *Sarum Sketches*). They are quite amusing. I have grown tremendously fond of him, and of most of the other kids. I do feel so sorry for the little beggars sometimes. Tho' I must say that they have few cares, and are, generally, a very happy lot.... If you could only see Salisbury Close and the Cathedral in the sunlight!" (CPC p.66).

The explanation of 'Ooce' was simply the boy's habit of exclaiming 'OO, Sir' at every opportunity! Howells has taken six of the boy's moods and written a short cameo sketch of each: *The Ooce March*; *The Drudge talks to himself*; *The Drudge forgotten*; *Ooce reads 'Arabian Nights'*; *Ooce at leisure*; and *Charades*. Stylistically the pieces show Howells's developing interest in harmonic colour and underline further his interest in miniature forms. There is still the air of the innocent 'Christopher Robin' about them – but perhaps in the reflection or portrayal of this small boy it is appropriate here. His personality is easily read through these colourful pieces and he was obviously a child of extremes of mood, reflective and apparently lonely, but also capable of great excitement and sensitivity. In all this Howells will perhaps have seen something of his own personality which must be part of the reason for his empathy with the boy.

As his time came to resign from Salisbury, so too, came the end of his College student career. It had been a dazzlingly successful one and is reflected in his list of prizes: the Manns Memorial Prize (1914), Sullivan Composition Prize (1914); Grove Scholarship (1914); Worshipful Company of Musicians Silver Medal (1915); The Tagore Gold Medal (1915); Bruce Scholarship (1916); the Organ Extemporisation Prize (1916) and the Dove Prize (1916); all these in addition to being six-times winner of the Director's History Essay Prize. Here was a remarkable achievement by any standards.

From January 1915 to March 1917 he also wrote regularly for the London arts paper *The Athenaeum*. This was done mostly in order to earn himself some money, and was something he described later as making him "tired of music as a daily and nightly boredom" (PH p.11). Whatever he felt about the drudgery of deadlines, however, it did serve to hone his literary style. As Eric Blom points out in the 1954 Grove Dictionary, Howells could have contributed significantly to the field of musical criticism if he had not been so strenuously occupied in other ways.

"Strenuously occupied" seems to sum up Howells's life. He was an inveterate worker and was under doctors' orders to stop, to rest, and to aid any possible recovery by reducing his self-inflicted workload. It must not be forgotten that Howells was still under a death sentence, and although the six-month threat was long past, no one knew how long the radium treatment being administered in almost complete ignorance would be effective.

Howells's resignation from Salisbury rendered him penniless and threw him back on the generosity of friends, sympathetic teachers and family. Help, however, came in the form of an unsolicited application to the Carnegie Trust made by Dr (later Sir) Henry Hadow, a noted educationist and, early on, composer. He wrote on Howells's behalf to ask the Trust to bend its rules in order to support him during the coming period of time in which he would not be able to earn his own living. The application letter he wrote is illuminating:

> I am very much distressed to hear that Mr H Howells, to whom one of the Carnegie awards was made last month (*Piano Quartet*), is very seriously ill, and that the doctor prescribes a period of complete rest as the only hope of recovery. This would be sad enough in any case; under the present circumstances it is really a disaster. Mr Howells has, I believe, no private means; he had just obtained his first official appointment, which he is now obliged to resign, and it seems wholly impossible that he should be able to carry out the doctor's instructions without very material assistance. Now in all my experience I do not think I have ever come across any young English musician of such remarkable promise.... Could the Carnegie Trust make a special grant, say, for a short term of years, in order to tide him over the difficult time until he is sufficiently recovered to take up his career?...
>
> Two possible objections might be brought forward: both, I think, can be met. First, that the Trust is concerned with objects of national importance, not of personal welfare. With this I agree, but I would urge that Howells's life *is* a matter of national importance. I am not asking for his sake so much as for the sake of future British Art, to which, if I am not wholly mistaken, he is better able to contribute than any man of his age now living.... I do most sincerely hope that you will be able to do something for a man on whom so much of the future of British music seems to me to depend.
>
> (CPC p.23)

This remarkable testimonial resulted in the Carnegie Trust awarding Howells a grant of £150 a year, then a substantial sum, for three years from 1 July 1917. In the words of the Trust Minutes, "it was decided to employ Mr Howells at a suitable salary in connexion

with the editing of Tudor and Elizabethan music, and that arrangements should be made with Dr Terry to that end. It is understood
that Dr Terry would very much welcome the suggestion" (ibid).

This was manna from heaven for both Howells and Terry who
had known and respected each other since 1912, and gave Howells
the opportunity to further his interest in music of the period and
give material assistance to Terry in his great proselytising cause.

The idea of the doctors being obeyed in terms of any reduction in
his outpouring of new works was obviously anathema to Howells.
This period was one of the most creative of his life, and the white
heat of inspiration (which may, of course, have had something to do
with the uncertainty of his survival hanging over him) gave us some
of his most outstanding early works. These included his *Fantasy
String Quartet*, a one-movement work in several sections, which
won the 1917 Cobbett Phantasy Competition. This event had been
set up to encourage British composers to breathe new life into the
Elizabethan Phantasy. Howells's quartet was summed up by the
composer himself in diary notes made in 1919: "Influence of Folk-
music is paramount in this. But here again is a compromise. I am a
'modern' in this, but a Britisher too! One of my best works, I think....
No break; tho' there are two distinct moods, the first much more
subjective than the second."

The 'compromise' can be read in various ways; he takes a view
on the constituents of folk idiom. There is something of Vaughan
Williams's *The Lark Ascending* in the free-wheeling first violin part
over a static chordal accompaniment with which the work begins
and which recurs at various points. (VW's work was written in 1914,
put away during the war, and then revised for its first performance
in 1920. Howells, therefore, could not have heard the work). The
melody, whilst indebted to folk idiom, is Howells's own, and the
music is absolutely in line with the 'mood' music discussed earlier.
There is also the 'modern' view of modality which was much
favoured by composers of the period and the approach to form.

The work underlines the principal problem which the 'pastoral'
composers faced and which their critics cite repeatedly. It is the crisis
of identity which comes of a marriage between a free folk-idiom which
has as its two constituent parts a bracing country dance element and

a wistful rambling tunefulness. These entail stricter dictates of formal requirements and a homogeneity of harmonic language and style. Howells's quartet somehow manages to get close to answering these problems, and there is no doubt that his remarkable sixth sense for mood creation lifts the whole work onto a different plane at those moments when recitative, improvisation, call it what you will, gives the work extraordinary elasticity and freedom.

Another work based on the one-movement principle is the first *Sonata for violin and piano*. At this time, for no apparent reason except perhaps his friendship with Sybil Eaton, one of the finest violinists of the day, Howells wrote a considerable amount of music for that instrument including two Sonatas in quick succession and of deeply differing natures. This first *Sonata* is extremely important, however, as its form is experimental and will reappear later on in relation to his second *Piano Concerto*.

> The object of my First Sonata... was to experiment in a new form of sonata; a form which, though without break from beginning to end, should establish three definite moods; and attain *unity* from a use of themes common to all three movements in varied rhythms and keys, and *diversity* from the careful metamorphosis of the themes to suit contrasted moods. I conceive the value of such a form to be in this: that while it ensures a logical growth *as a whole*; and while it preserves in itself the contrast of line and of colour which is provided by the sequence of three separate movements as commonly adopted in the Sonata or Symphony; it at the same time draws all three moods under a closer, unified spell. It becomes more a triple mood... [rather] than a succession of three more intensely contrasted and separated moods.
> (CPC p.448)

The result is highly successful, and shows Howells's sleight of hand at a remarkable and ingenious rethinking of existing formal methods. It also demonstrates his ability to work on a bigger canvas than he had perhaps been willing to do in his recent past. The work was performed in Birmingham, Leeds and London, and Howells noted wryly that "The 'critics' in the latter city were much disgusted by the new ideas of form; in Birmingham they were much keener on it; and in Leeds there was real understanding!!" (ibid p.71)

Whether or not *The Times* reviewer was one of those Howells deemed to have been 'disgusted' is not recorded, but it is interesting to note the measured criticism. "The Sonata is not what we have hitherto called a Sonata, but a 'Contemplation' with a moment of rhapsody in it. It is English in its independence of thought and a certain modesty and scorn of advertisement; for instance, in about the sixth bar it is off in G major (the Sonata is in E), but it does not make any fuss about it" (PH p.140).

The second *Violin Sonata* (in E flat) was also composed in 1917 and is written on an altogether bigger scale than the first. If anything it presents a greater enigma than that original work. In the E flat *Sonata* Howells returns to the more standard format of a four-movement work. Like the first *Sonata* it was later revised in 1919. It presents interesting problems for the biographer in that Howells wrote a note with the manuscript to the effect that it had "been discarded by the composer". This is a rare thing to find with his music for, although we know that he withdrew various works during the course of his life (including the two *Piano Concertos* and the *Pastoral Rhapsody*) he never went as far as destroying the manuscripts. In fact the only time that he is known to have actually done this was after a dinner at Trinity College, Cambridge when he dined with A.E. Housman, who spent the whole evening railing against composers who set his poems to music. Special invective was reserved for Vaughan Williams who had cut two verses of *Is my team ploughing* in his setting ("How would he feel if I cut two bars of his music?"). Afterwards Howells destroyed the songs he had taken expressly to show Housman. This is a tragic loss considering the quality of music he was composing at this period, but typical of his sensitivity.

The second *Violin Sonata* was another advance, formally, though in different ways from the first. Howells said of it: "Four movements in this. Last two are linked. I know nothing in violin-and-piano music that is at all like the 3rd movement (a Scherzo). Certain themes appear in various guises in *all* the movements".

The *Daily Telegraph* critic made constructive remarks following its first London performance on 18 February 1919:

> That he is a man with something fresh and interesting to say and a distinctly individual way of saying it, Mr Herbert Howells has shown on not a few occasions.... It is true that there are moments

in this Sonata when one feels that he is trying to be original for originality's sake, or that his material is not quite worth his immensely elaborate and ingenious treatment of it; but these moments are entirely outnumbered by those in which he gives us music that is extremely worth having... The Sonata is not without its faults, but it is a work of considerable accomplishment and still greater promise.

Which young composer of real talent has not had to deal with the barbed comment about technique versus inspiration? One might think of Britten's mauling at the hands of the press over just this point. Howells's diary on the day after the first performance revealingly says, "The critics were rather 'pleasant', but they can't forgive me for being still 'one of the youngest of our composers'. They forget in how few years many men have done their life's work." It is genuinely difficult to think why Howells decided to withdraw this work, which is strong, passionate and committed. It is quite likely that it was written in response to John Ireland's immensely successful second *Violin Sonata* performed by Alfred Sammons and William Murdoch to such acclaim. Knowing Howells's sensitivity, it is also highly likely that when it did not attract similar acclaim he would rather that it were out of circulation than living its life in the shadow of a successful work by a rival contemporary. It also has to be said that despite Howells's claims as to its originality, its formal ideas are very similar to Ireland's, and Ireland's idea of thematic recurrence between movements is also taken up by Howells. That said, Howells's is a much more 'modern' work in its language, style and feeling. Ireland's could be said to be tainted with a certain sentimentality which is a trait of which Howells is never musically guilty. It has already been noted that Howells found pathos something which moved him deeply, but pathos is a very different thing from sentiment. The muscularity of this *Sonata* is far removed from the pastoral mood-creation of the *Fantasy String Quartet* and maybe was something which Howells did not want to perpetuate. Added to other sensitivities was Stanford's dislike of the work about which he said "I'm afraid I'm getting old, dear boy... I can't accustomize my nostrils to these modern stinks". As Howells said in response: "I had rather I had pleased him" although, in fact, he took little notice of the issue.

By this time Stanford was losing his hold on his young composer-pupils, at least as far as teacher-pupil relations were concerned.

Howells never strayed far from the small-scale character pieces which were becoming a hallmark of his output. *Puck's Minuet*, for instance, an orchestral miniature also from 1917, was commissioned by Herbert Brewer for his Gloucestershire Orchestral Society and dedicated to his daughter. Howells, whose ear was legendary, and who was capable of writing the most complex counterpoint in the middle of a crowded hotel lobby, wrote the whole piece in one three-hour sitting in Reading Station waiting room whilst waiting for his train to Gloucester. The work was written straight out in full score.

So successful was the first London performance, given by Sir Hamilton Harty with the LSO in March 1919, that it had to be repeated straightaway. Howells was unable to attend owing to continuing illness and he therefore watched the press the next day with especial interest. "I had *Puck* in mind all day, thinking of how it would fare at the Queen's Hall.... To know its fate meant waiting till tomorrow morning." Then the moment arrived: "And on this first day of Lent I learned from the *Daily Telegraph* and the *Times* and all the other press, how the little *Puck* had so delighted the people gathered together at the Queen's Hall that it had to be repeated immediately... a most unusual occurrence." The *Times*' notice said "It is all as clear as a summer sky and as light as feather.... He has a true instinct for the moment of repose which brings the agitation of thinly written parts into focus".

Whilst all this was going on work was progressing with Terry at Westminster Cathedral on his work for the Carnegie Trust. His relationship with Dorothy Dawe was also deepening to the point where they could announce their engagement. Howells indicates when this was to be in a passionate letter written at Salisbury on 1 April 1917, the anniversary of a recital at Newnham, Gloucestershire on 2 April 1913 when Howells first fully fell under Dorothy's spell:

> What patience we two poor things have had to exercise, even to come to the happy state of engagement! That state ought rightly to have been accomplished tomorrow, which is our blessed day. But it shall no later (after the 12th inst) that my opportunity and bashfulness allow.
>
> (CPC p.65)

It is perhaps with some difficulty that one remembers that the Great War was still raging all around them, in the midst of all this positive work, his success and with a fulfilling relationship shortly to blossom into marriage. Certainly the powers-that-be were absolutely delighted and relieved that at least one of their protégés was not in the firing line, although Howells's ultimate fate with regard to his illness was still not yet known. There also hung over him the possibility of some sort of military service. Parry, ever helpful in these matters, wrote sending a testimonial which he hoped would help exempt Howells from any call-up. "I can't think the military authorities will carry you off.... If they do – well – it's a cruel lot for one of your disposition, but in this country the military spirit is ruthless and undiscriminating.... I can only hope, eagerly, that they won't take you" (CPC p.18). In fact they never did, but inevitably the feeling that he had the soft option while his friends and colleagues were enduring the most appalling conditions in the trenches and elsewhere made him extremely sensitive to his position.

A letter to a local photographer in Lydney written on 16 April 1918 indicates just how he felt: "My dear Mr Coe, I'm sure you won't mind my asking you to take my photo and the printed notice out of your front window now. They have had an undeservedly good innings there now: and with news as it is, and military thought and exigency so uppermost, there is perhaps reason why so absolutely a useless person as myself should not be in any way too prominent in the thoughts of an oft-times thoughtless public!" On hearing the news of Howells's Carnegie Trust grant after resigning Salisbury, Gurney once again found it difficult to contain his envy: "You are indeed queerly treated of the gods to be cast up again so high after so great a fall. £150 a year as sub-editor and at such a job! O bon! (By the way, in February they raised my yearly emolument from £18/4/0 to £22/5/0)" (CPC p.45). He finishes this letter "Will no-one do your Concerto again? That has been rather a shock to me, that such a fine piece of music should appear and attract so little notice. Still, cheer up! For if the worst comes to the worst you shall get a word in my Biography" (ibid). That must really have stung, and yet the motivation for it will have been entirely clear to Howells. The surprise in some respects is that he should have written to Gurney with all the fine details of his luck. This surely smacks either of insecurity (never far beneath the surface) or point-scoring. Either way it emphasises the point made earlier about strained relations between the two friends.

One friend and fellow student at the RCM of whom Howells was extremely fond was Francis Purcell Warren ('Bunny' of 'The B's'). Warren was a viola player and was killed at the battle of Mons in 1917. It was in his memory that Howells wrote (or revised and removed from a recent *Suite for Strings*) one of his most remarkable works, the *Elegy* for viola solo, string quartet and string orchestra. In his autobiography published only shortly before his death in 1996, the composer Alan Ridout, a pupil of Howells at the RCM from 1951, remembered a fascinating incident which took place in one of Howells's "charismatic and incomparable" lectures (AR p.41). A few days after the death of King George VI Howells spoke about the subject of mourning.

> The lecture culminated in something like a testament; so far as I know, and simply by chance, only I fully understood it. He said that he was going to play a recording of a work – what it was, and who it was by, was of no consequence – which summed up all that could be stated in music about death. His exact words were: "If there is a better expression of the music of mourning, I have yet to hear it." I happened to know the recording and the work, though I did not let on, and thus became, from that moment, part of the conspiracy. It was his own *Elegy*.
> (ibid p.42-43)

Ridout refers to Warren again in a later chapter specifically about Howells:

> There is no doubt in my mind that he loved Francis Purcell Warren. He had a snapshot of him on his mantelpiece, standing together with Leon Goossens.... Once he stood before the picture gradually becoming inarticulate with grief. After a long silence he said "He was *everything* to me" and sobbed, then swiftly pulled himself together.
> (ibid p.55)

Ridout is at pains to point out that this was no homosexual love, but a deeply close bond as is often only found between friends of the same sex who are, as often as not, happily married. The *Elegy* is certainly a striking testimonial to this friendship where there was no such tribute to Gurney following his death, even though Gurney had featured prominently enough in Howells's music over the years, most notably in the *Piano Quartet*.

At this time death was all around him and not by any means just war-related death. Two people who meant the world to him, and in their own way were both fathers to him, died within a year of each other. Hubert Parry who died on 21 October 1918 was "an irreparable loss", as Parry's son-in-law, the baritone Harry Plunket Greene, said in a letter to Howells a few days after his death. More fundamental even than this, though, was the death of his own father.

Oliver Howells had gone into a long terminal decline after his business had failed and he had brought disgrace (as he saw it) upon the family. He was never the same again, and after a while went into a slow decline, locking himself away, refusing comfort or help. He died on 21 September 1919 and Howells made the following entry in his diary:

> A sadly memorable day for all of us: for my dear father, suddenly taken with a seizure at 9.15 a.m., lingered (unconscious, thank heaven!) only until 2.15 in the afternoon, and passed from us then.... It was to a Bath Villa with its eyes shut that I came (at 4 o'clock pm) by motor cycle side-car... only to realise that father was already dead.... Nature was in its loveliest mood today; and it seemed to me a glorious day on which to pass out of this life.... It was such a Sunday afternoon as he loved always in his hale and hearty days, for a walk with one or more of us boys of his.... Those walks, and his delightful companionship, he charming entertainment for us at flagging moments... and all the greater innumerable kindnesses came back in crowded memories to us today, and one felt more acutely than ever what we had lost in him. A sad day... most of all for mother – poor dear!... a great wrench for her to bear.... Those at Bath Villa today were Mother, Winnie, Florrie, Will, Howard and Trissie, with little Joyce and Mary.

The great sadness was that Oliver had not lived long enough to see his youngest son happily married to the girl he had courted and loved since 1913.

Before we reach that milestone in Howells's life, however, we must examine some other works written at this time which furthered the public's feeling of his celebrity, and the profession's view that he was the leading talent of his generation. Principal among them is the *Rhapsodic Quintet* for clarinet and string quartet completed in June 1919. Howells said of the work that there was "a mystic feeling about the whole thing", and in a diary entry for 1 March: "I have long, ponderous thoughts on problems of Musical Form... hours spent in an easy chair, fire-gazing, form-thinking. Most of it focused on the Clarinet Quintet. We want new experiments in form, and a sympathetic consideration of them when they are made."

The *Quintet* is another single movement work, though, yet again with a different approach from the *Fantasy String Quartet* or the first *Violin Sonata*. This time Howells takes two musical ideas which are freely developed throughout: the first is energetic and the second a beautifully lyrical melody. The real magic of this work, though, is the serenely peaceful music which brings it to its conclusion. A wonderful example of Howells the mood-conjurer.

1918 was a remarkable year in Howells's development. Aged twenty-six he was working at a fever pitch, and a comment Gerald Finzi made about Gurney's setting of *Sleep* after his first hearing of it in York at Bairstow's house has some resonance with Howells in this period. Finzi wrote that it was "not being wise after the event to say that one can feel an incandescence in Gurney's songs that tells of something burning too brightly to last, such as you see in the filament of an electric bulb before it burns out" (GF p.393). It was, after all, the last couple of years before Howells was married and settled with a regular job and the necessity of earning a living which would support wife and family. These last days of 'freedom' were prolific to a degree almost unimaginable in a man still under some sort of sentence of death.

Besides chamber and orchestral music, he was also continuing the canon of important organ works which he had begun with such conspicuous success with the early set of *Psalm Preludes* and the *first Rhapsody*. He now completed the set of three projected *Rhapsodies* of which the second and third had Howells declaring how glad he was to be "getting away from the church!". They were "serious attempts at a more freely-expressed music for the instrument". Both these pieces are intensely dramatic and are among his most obvious 'troubled times' pieces. The *third Rhapsody*, as has become well-known, was written in one all-night sitting at Bairstow's house in York when Howells was kept awake by a Zeppelin raid. The turbulent music reflects the drama of the occasion.

Explaining his approach to composing these works Howells said: "The modern organ is a marvellous colour-medium, and demands a suitable idiom for making full use of its resources. It can give bursts of colour that are not possible on the orchestra. Why, then, not take advantage of its capacity? It's absurd to think that only contrapuntal writing is suitable for the organ. And even if it were, we can't compete with Bach!" (TMT).

Procession for solo piano came to life through a dream in which Howells dreamt that "he was in Nizhny-Novgorod and there, in a complex of streets, he became aware of a processional movement approaching, gathering momentum and then suddenly disappearing" (CPS p.68). The piece is monothematic and is an extraordinary exercise in cumulative building and sudden dissipation. Originally conceived for orchestra Howells felt ill-equipped to orchestrate it to his satisfaction in 1917, and it had to wait until 1922 before he felt sufficiently confident to translate the relative monochrome of the piano into the glorious technicolour of a large orchestra.

To those who know Howells only as a composer of choral and organ music it will have probably have come as something of a surprise to see how much of a fringe activity Howells's contact with choral music seems to be at this stage of his life. However, there were two important works written between 1918 and 1920 which point strongly not only to his intuitive affinity with voices, but to his absolutely personal style in this field. The first was his earliest setting of a *Magnificat and Nunc Dimittis in G*. This, whilst not in the fully-fledged impressionistic style of his later canticle settings, has much of the inherent rapture of the later style wrapped up in a more conservative language. Of greater significance and world-wide popularity to this day are the three carol-anthems *Here is the little door*; *Sing Lullaby*; and *A Spotless Rose*. With these miniature masterpieces Howells nailed his true colours to the mast and staked his claim to be Stanford's linear successor in the highly sophisticated process of revolutionising the music of the Anglican church. At a single stroke, these three small-scale Christmas pieces lit a beacon over a new pathway which would inspire church musicians and congregations from then onwards. The light shines as brightly today as it did in 1918.

Here is the little door sets a tender little poem by G.K. Chesterton, who suggested it to Howells. *Sing Lullaby* was the last to be written (1920) and was, once again, set to a poem suggested by its author, the Gloucestershire poet F.W. Harvey, friend of both Gurney and Howells. *A Spotless Rose*, the most celebrated of the set, was written

> after idly watching some shunting from the window of a cottage... in Gloucester which overlooked the Midland Railway. In an upstairs room I looked out on iron railings and the main Bristol-Gloucester railway line, with shunting trucks bumping and banging. I wrote it for and dedicated it to my Mother – it always moves me when I hear it, just as if it were written by someone else.
> (CPC p.399)

So wrote Howells about this extraordinary little piece. At its end is a magical cadence of which Howells's friend the composer Patrick Hadley said:

> O Herbert, that cadence to *A Spotless Rose* is not merely 'one of those things'. Brainwave it certainly is, but it is much more than that. It is a stroke of genius. I should like, when my time comes, to pass away with that magical cadence. I expect you'll say you hadn't to think, it was already there.
> (ibid)

Patrick Hadley's off-the-cuff remark reminds us yet again of the Celtic sensibility never far beneath the surface, and of 'things ordained'. If anything was ordained, however, it would seem that Howells's friendship with the poet Walter de la Mare was. De la Mare and Howells spoke the same language, both had Celtic backgrounds, and both responded to things numinous in a quite uncanny way. Here too was a poet who, unlike the dictatorial and unsympathetic Housman, not only understood the need for composers to set words to music, but positively encouraged it. De la Mare had been a chorister at St Paul's Cathedral. The main meeting point between the two men was a common language with which both had complete empathy. In his copy of *A Tribute to Walter de la Mare* on his seventy-fifth birthday Howells had put inside the front jacket a cutting from the *Daily Telegraph* in which Rachel Trickett was reviewing the *Best Stories of Walter de la Mare*. In her article Trickett makes some telling points: "his mastery of the bizarre, the strange, the haunted"; that he "loved children and understood them"; that:

> Commonplace life, the ordinariness of existence, is suddenly lit up by the perception of truth; the meanest things become lovely; the commonest responses extraordinary. Only a writer of genuine imaginative genius can achieve this, and de la Mare possesses such a genius. It operated in narrow limits, but he was the most fluent and fertile of writers in prose and verse.

In his book *Sensibility and English Song* Stephen Banfield notes in his chapter on Georgian poetry and Georgian Music that "the interwar ambience was primarily one of lyrical retreat;.... Put simply... a retreat to the country and a retreat to the fantasy world of childhood. The first characterises the Georgian poets in general, the second the most distinguished of their number, Walter de la Mare" (SES p.208). The interesting thing is that almost any adjective one chooses to apply to de la Mare can equally be applied to Howells, and in the latter's setting of the former's poem *King David* the perfection of the match is personified. The size and scope of the present book prevents what would be a fascinating study of the parallel paths of these two creative men. One only has to examine the songs in *Peacock Pie*, the huge cycle of songs designated *A Garland for de la Mare*, and *King David*, to see a remarkable and moving partnership of equals whose collective genius has given us, in *King David*, at least one miniature masterpiece.

Banfield points out that de la Mare "possessed a genius for telling stories in verse. This was primarily a function of his entering into the world of children.... *King David*, from *Peacock Pie*, has nothing to do with children... we share in the mysterious moods of a great king" (SES p.226). Howells said "I'm prouder to have written 'King David' than almost anything else of mine – de la Mare once said he didn't want anyone else to set it" (CPS p.16).

FIVE
A Turbulent Period (1919-1926)

Reading Howells's first diary kept from the start of 1919 is to become swept up in a fast-moving story. Every page is filled with action, reminiscence, reflection, reaction, and hopes for things to come. Two things strike the reader immediately; one is that the diary is intended to be read; the other is its stilted literary style. A typical example occurs on 28 January when Howells goes from Gloucester to Oxford.

> It was 2.15pm when I got there, and found Henry Ley with his choristers at Ch.Ch. [Christ Church]. I called at Queen's, but Mr Gonshaw was absent. So I found W.T. Walton in his rooms at The House (local name for Christ Church), busy with his highly-coloured chords. He shewed me the first movement of a Pianoforte Qtte. If he gets in the right hands, he'll be an interesting musical personage.

There is a constant feeling that we are intended to be impressed by his range of acquaintances, his constant travel, his acceptance and welcome at the high tables of Oxbridge colleges, and the implied breadth of his reputation. A slightly earlier entry for 16 January is equally revealing:

> A day in an old haunt – the R.C.M. I attended the General Meeting of the R.C.M. Union. There was Dr. Allen in the chair (for the first time here), weighed down with thoughts of the difficult waiting called upon to succeed to fine a being as Sir Hubert [Parry].... There was a big and famous gathering.... And I did wonders in the matter of handing round the tea.

The sub-text here is revealing; that he was privy to Dr Allen's thoughts; that he was one of the 'famous gathering'; and that he was jolly magnanimous in 'handing round the tea'.

This is not intended as a rather cruel dissection of a young man's personality, it is merely a footnote that, as Sir Thomas Armstrong remembered, Howells "was a complex character, and a real under-standing of him will not be easy to reach, or entirely acceptable to those who were fond of him" (CPC p.129). As such, it is important to remember a number of things which contributed to that complex mix of heredity and environment which went to make up his mature personality. There was his supportive but disastrously unworldly family and their social isolation in Lydney; his being a big fish in a small pond from a very early age; his small stature; his remarkable good looks; his complete technical assurance and early musical suc-cess; his winning charm; and his apparently outgoing nature which actually hid both a strongly depressive streak, a natural shyness, and a debilitatingly advanced sensitivity to criticism. All these things, and others besides, went into his music, his writing, his public speaking, adjudicating, examining, and personal dealings with peo-ple. In fact it was a white-hot cauldron of conflicting signals which spilled over at various points in his life, and was otherwise more or less kept in check through the safety valve of his composition and his few close friendships with Arthur Benjamin and 'Bunny' Warren (in particular), Arthur Bliss and, on a different plane, Dorothy Dawe.

The references to Dorothy throughout this narrative diary are always soft-edged, and there is invariably a 'second subject' change of character in his writing style when she appears. It is almost as if he is living out a fantasy through her. 31 January 1919:

> Parton Lane is paved with musical thoughts: and cows and sheep walk on them and vainly imagine that they walk on stones and mud. This morning I saw string-quartet tunes along the way... In Gloucester I bought lemons, eggs, flowers, and books for a sick girl, and came back along Tune Lane.

Parton Lane is actually Pirton Lane at the foot of Chosen Hill.

> 3 February:
> I extemporised mad absurdities for D... she repaid me with

laughter. And I pottered about the Tune Lane, in the dark and the damp, with trees like ghosts, and cows and horses like dimly-seen terrible monsters. Dear things!

The diary also gives us a clue to budding friendships with other women. One gets the strongest impression that he likes being surrounded by titled people, and it is therefore perhaps not surprising that when he is introduced to Lady Olga Montagu on 18 January at a "music party at the Scott's (Marion Scott) in 92 Westbourne Terrace" at which Sybil Eaton played his four new violin pieces and Thalben-Ball played the piano in a performance of his *Piano Quartet*, he "liked her". The next day he was practising with Sybil Eaton at Viscountess de Vesci's house in Bruton Street for a concert that evening, the first half of which consisted of his first *Violin Sonata*, *Five Songs* (perhaps the ones now known as *In Green Ways* in the pre-revised version of 1915) sung by Harry Plunket Greene, and the four new violin pieces "in all of which I was the miserable pianist. There was a big crowd. Thereafter I went to supper in Oxford Street with Benjamin, Gurney, A.C. Trimmer & Erlebach for companions. I hate publicity!" Which comment should probably be treated in the same manner as 'I did wonders in handing round the tea'.

10 February:
My interest in life was suddenly revived at 4.30 p.m. by a letter from Lady Olga Montagu, and one (written by her hand) from 'Carolus'. Carolus addressed me in poetry. I promptly retaliated in a specialised way, and so there came into existence the quaint 'Carolus Cantat', and this hee-haw will live with O.M. and H.H all their days.

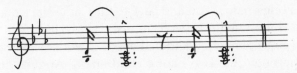

Olga Montagu, the sister of the Earl of Sandwich, became a very important person in Howells's life. At this point when he was poor and struggling to get known she was extremely generous to him, giving him a piano and a gold watch, and becoming a sort of unofficial 'patron'. Ursula Howells described her as a "formidable and masculine-looking woman – an intellectual who enjoyed long conversations with my father" (UH/PS). Later on she was Michael's godmother and later on still was exceptionally generous in helping Howells buy the house 3 Beverley Close, Barnes which was his home from 1946 until his death.

Space does not permit more 'general' digging through the diary, but the picture grows of a young man very much in popular vogue, the darling of society parties, the pet of the smart set and, seemingly, a considerable flirt with it. One further reminiscence concerns the marvellous portrait drawing by Sir William Rothenstein which now hangs in the Senior Common Room at the RCM. On 20 December Howells writes:

> The real business of my visit to Rothenstein was accomplished this morning, when I sat for my portrait. In two hours (or little more) he made a marvellous drawing; and caught me in one of my rare 'càlénde' moods. He demonstrated in this drawing his fast-held theory that a real portrait is essentially similar to a good lyric: it is a thing of intense and localised mood.

On May 24 1920 Howells's (much less forthcoming) diary indicates a visit to Canon Cheesman at Twigworth. It is likely that this was with Dorothy to make arrangements for their forthcoming wedding. In the coming weeks the couple spent a good deal of time in the village and on Tuesday 3 August he notes: "To wed D at Twigworth 9.45 a.m. Please God! A most beautiful day for us in Gloucestershire and at Wells where we arrived (Swan Hotel) at 4 p.m. and were at once 'discovered'." 4 August: "The rain came again. Walked along Bristol Road and back to the Cathedral – rained relentlessly. We communed much." 5 August: "Corrected proofs of 'Gogy o Gay'" [no trace now]. Wandered about Cheddar Caves and rocks in the afternoon like two happy children." 7 August: "Left Wells at 9.45 a.m. Arrived Soudley 3.20pm. Walked to Blakeney on shopping expedition." 8 August: "Walked to Viney Hill in morning. Soudley keeps its church door locked – The Littledean road is hard – we turned back." 9 August: "'Merry Eye' occupied me after a brief walk on the hill tops. D and I lagged(?) over the Bailey Hill and saw miles of the Cotswolds and Severn. 'Merry Eye' occupied the evening." And so the diary goes on in more or less detail telling of a happy and unusual honeymoon lasting until Saturday the twenty-first, most of which was spent at Box Cottage, Soudley in Gloucestershire not far from Lydney.

The 'unusual' element concerned Howells's orchestral work *Merry Eye* referred to in the diary. Howells told the story that he and Dorothy got on the train from Gloucester to Wells at which point he opened *The Times* to see the announcement that he was to write a work for that year's Promenade Concerts. The way Howells told it (very convincingly) was that "I didn't know, but a letter from Henry [Wood] had gone astray apparently. I had never got it, and he had assumed that Howells would do it, and Howells did do it, but I scarcely saw my wife during our honeymoon. I used to sit up until 2 and 2.30 in the morning. Fancy a man doing that on his honeymoon!" (BBC/Prizeman).

In fact this was an entirely apocryphal story for correspondence survives between Howells and Wood agreeing the details. Presumably Howells concocted the story as a face-saver and to add a little local colour, which it certainly did! It speaks volumes for Howells's confidence in his ability that he could leave the writing of even a short orchestral work until only a month before its first performance (30 September). It is also perhaps telling that he must have packed manuscript paper in preparation. The indications are that it was written straight out in full score as, when they left Box Cottage they both signed the visitors' book and Herbert wrote a full-score section of the work into the book.

As a postscript to this happy interlude it is interesting to hear Marion Scott describe the musical content of the wedding service which was most unusual. She wrote about it in the *Christian Science Monitor* (a paper published in Boston, USA) early in September:

> Several well-known British musicians have recently been associated in a gift to Herbert Howells, the composer, and his wife, which is as charming as it is characteristic. The gift takes the form of a collection of original tunes in the folk-song style, each composer having either contributed a new one, or else sent a quotation from some work of his already written... they have

been played... by George Thalben-Ball, the brilliant young acting organist of the Temple Church... Thalben-Ball wove these tunes... into what was nominally a Fantasia, but which... was also an eloquent and moving oration upon the ideas of love and peace.

(CSM 9.20)

She goes on to describe the contributions from Stanford, Holst, Howells himself (the lovely *Chosen* tune), Parry, Richard Terry, Thalben-Ball, Rupert Erlebach and back via a reprise of Holst, Parry and finally Herbert's tune again.

Before his marriage Howells had been appointed to the teaching staff of the Royal College in April. So 1920 signalled the end not only of his literal honeymoon, but also his honeymoon of carefree youth and with it, too, his total focus on composition. At this point, despite the outward happiness of his life, a small flag should be hung at half mast to mark the moment at which other pressures began to crowd his career, to such an extent that he was never really to fulfil that promise which Sir Henry Hadow had so eloquently hoped would see him leading the pack of British composers, and in which Stanford had invested so much faith. It is a serious moment, for despite undisputed masterpieces to come, there is no doubt that as a composer Howells never really fulfilled the great hopes invested in him and for which he was uniquely equipped, however outwardly successful his professional life might have appeared.

After their marriage Herbert and Dorothy took flat 44 in Castelnau at Barnes on the river Thames near Hammersmith Bridge. Barnes was then to be home for the rest of their lives. It was an ideal spot, far enough removed from central London to feel 'countrified', close to the river with all its atmosphere, yet close enough also to the city and to the RCM to be entirely convenient for entertainment and work.

Howells's relations with Edward Elgar had gradually warmed into a friendship based on mutual respect. Elgar was, of course, revered in Three Choirs country and everywhere else, and ever since Howells had been associated with Gloucester he had been introduced to Elgar on numerous occasions. Famously, he told of a final loss of patience with the great man who affected once more not to know him: "I am fed up with being introduced to Sir Edward Elgar" was the outburst from a very young and bold Howells. But it paid off, for after this Elgar could not do enough for him, and in 1920 summoned Bliss, Eugene Goossens and Howells to a meeting which in the event Howells could not attend. All three were commissioned to write a work for the 1922 Gloucester Festival. Bliss wrote his *Colour Symphony*, Goossens's work was a setting of de la Mare's 'Silence', and Howells's offering was *Sine Nomine, A Phantasy*.

Sine Nomine is an extremely unusual concept and is interesting on several levels. First, it is scored for large orchestra, two wordless soloists (soprano and tenor) and wordless choir – of which more shortly. Its very name, meaning 'without name', conjures up resonances of the 'in nomine' of the Elizabethan period, and yet with the slight mystery of a little modern enigma to add spice to its mood. Thus, without using the same idea as Vaughan Williams in his *Tallis Fantasia*, Howells nevertheless marries ancient and modern in a way which was to become increasingly his hallmark. Add to that the contours of the work's principal melodic idea which harks back to plainsong in its freedom, shape, and apparently never-ending flow, and the 'reverie' of two floating wordless voices, and you come up with an extraordinarily original recipe for what Howells described as a "spiritual meditation". It is an entirely original work, and it is no wonder that the performers were baffled by it, or that the singer Harry Plunket Greene asked Howells to give the soloists words just before the first performance. Howells was also obviously in two minds about this, and eventually decided to agree to give them words from the Vulgate. This was never put in the full score, and at its second performance in 1992 (when it was edited by the present author) the work was performed as originally intended, without words. The same uncertainty hung over the issue of the chorus. In the end Howells made the lower parts wordless, and gave the sopranos and altos the word 'ora' (pray) to sing.

The work was placed before *Elijah* on Tuesday 5 September and was therefore guaranteed an unsympathetic hearing. As the *Musical Times* reviewer said, "it was hardly discreet to put it before an *Elijah* audience, who would be unlikely to give it a very patient or intelligent hearing". The critic of the *Gloucester Journal*, however, was more positive when he said "Possibly with a more intimate acquaintance we should grow acclimatised to the atmosphere of this ultra-modern orchestration and become even more enamoured of it". But sadly, "intimate acquaintance" was not going to be the fate of this work.

Twelve days after that performance the Howells's first child, Ursula Mary, was born and Howells's diary notes that "The dear daughter came at 7.45 p.m."

In the meantime it is salutary to note to what extent Howells's writing had fallen away. After a last golden year in 1919 and some activity in 1920, there is little surviving evidence of much writing in 1921 (only one song, *Blaweary*, in fact), and in 1922 *Sine Nomine* stands out as being the one major advance besides the hugely successful orchestration of the 1918 piano work *Procession*. It must be said that no one knows how much was lost when the Howells's house was bombed in September 1940, but it is pretty clear that his growing demands in the areas of teaching, examining and adjudicating had taken a serious toll on his compositional output, and it is unlikely that much was destroyed which is not known about.

With reference to *Procession* it is illuminating to hear Alan Ridout's reminiscences:

> I have always been grateful for my first experience of the music of Herbert Howells. For a young boy who was a chorister and who played the piano, this introduction to his work was some-what unusual. In the summer of 1946, I was taken to my first Promenade Concert – I can remember the exact spot in the balcony where I and the friend of an aunt sat – each item on the programme enchanted me more than the last. Brahms conducted by Boult in the first half seemed wonderful enough; but the first performance of the suite from a ballet *Adam Zero*, by Arthur Bliss (then non-establishment and yet to be knighted), fairly galloped along under the sizzling baton of Constant Lambert. But it was the last piece, Howells's *Procession*, which crowned the evening and forever blessed the day for me. As that sombre melody, with its slightly sinister tread, swooshed its way round the large orchestra I was as moved and delighted as I had ever been.
> (AR p.41)

Another work which had a curious genesis was Howells's *In*

Gloucestershire string quartet. The origins of this work go right back to 1916 when Howells wrote a work which he described as "real Gloucestershire" (CSM 12.20) but absentmindedly left it on the train in which he was travelling between Gloucester and Lydney. No one could find the lost manuscript – the only one in existence – and thus matters rested until the autumn of 1919 when, quite unexpectedly, Howells began to remember themes from the work. As the *Christian Science Monitor* article about the work says:

> He decided to rewrite the quartet and had indeed begun it when fresh inspiration suddenly came to him. The old themes were discarded, new material flooded his thoughts, and in a fortnight of ceaseless work he finished the quartet.
> (ibid)

Sydney Grew, writing that article, gives a very detailed account of the work producing fanciful and yet intuitively sensitive insights into Howells's compositional process. One particularly interesting idea is that "while the general scheme is that of free sonata form, successfully and modernly handled, the themes and passages springing out of them are consistently expressed in dual waves. It is the parallelism of the Psalms: in which a short poetic statement immediately receives as a response an expansion of the same idea or one closely allied to it. Howells had no definite awareness of borrowing the ancient Hebraic form, but not long before the composition of *In Gloucestershire* he had been at work upon a set of Psalm-Preludes, and had so steeped himself in the Psalms that he unconsciously reproduced their structure in his music."

This 1920 version of the quartet was not the end of the story, however, and two more versions of the work exist at the RCM. On 8 January 1923 Howells notes in his diary: "Parts of String Quartet to be with Spencer Dyke by 6 p.m.". The version played by this group has a completely new first movement from that of the 1920 work. Howells was evidently still unhappy about aspects of the music and in the 1930s provided another major revision with new slow and final movements, the slow movement in particular being a tellingly beautiful, elegiac meditation.

Whatever the circuitous route to completion, *In Gloucestershire* remains a towering achievement and one of the most remarkable additions to the chamber music repertory by a British composer of this century.

In 1920 Howells had been signed up as an examiner for the Associated Board of the Royal Schools of Music, and he spent periods in each year following examining mainly youngsters who were working their way up the grading system. In 1923 he was still recuperating and regaining his strength after the prolonged radium treatment which had left him weak, but cured of the disease which had haunted him for so many years. In view of this the Board sent him on two foreign examining tours, one to South Africa in 1921, and the other in 1923 to Canada which it was hoped would help him to a full recovery.

Both trips were musically fruitful, but the second was particularly important, and had its expression in the *Violin Sonata no.3* in E minor (it is interesting how all three of Howells's *Violin Sonatas* are in the tonality of E). The importance of this work lies in its powerful response to a completely foreign stimulus, the Canadian Rockies. This was something so far from his experience that we should not be surprised when confronted with this new and vastly more dissonant style, a long way from the subtle portrayals of the gentle rolling countryside of his native Gloucestershire. This work is Howells's equivalent of Vaughan Williams's *Fourth Symphony* but without the torment of that work. The fascinating thing is to experience Howells's dilemma in the *Sonata's* opening bars. What should he do? How should he translate the awesome scale and beauty of such a scene as the Rockies into music? That Howells chose to do it through the medium of chamber music rather than what might have been a rather overblown orchestral score is also a telling point. But he does manage to achieve a wonderful sense of the scale and of the ruggedness of the scenery in music which Philip Radcliffe described as "fiercely dissonant (at least by the standards of the time)" (CPC p.214).

The other sizeable work from 1923 is the *Pastoral Rhapsody*, another work which Howells later withdrew. It is a rich evocation of nature, a true exercise in pastoral reflection, and one of Howells's biggest single-spans. At its opening it bears slightly too uncomfortably close a resemblance to Vaughan Williams's *Pastoral Symphony* which, finished in 1921, was very recent in Howells's experience. Howells was deeply moved and fascinated by this work of Vaughan Williams's, and wrote passionately in its defence in the face of its many contemporary detractors. There is no single work by another composer which so clearly defines Howells's own approach to composition (see Chapter 3).

A perceived problem with the *Pastoral Rhapsody* is a lack of real melodic invention – and a frequent resort to note-spinning which we noted as a "fault-line" as far back as the early 1911 *Organ Sonata*. Alan Ridout put both strengths and weaknesses very succinctly when he said "Howells's great strength as a composer was an ability to make a large continuous structure. He composed in large paragraphs. It is a rare gift and something which Stanford noted in him. He also had the ability to produce a saturated but luminous texture.... Where I felt he was weak at times was that his individual themes lacked strength of character" (AR p.54).

This is by no means a general trait, and it is perfectly possible to robustly defend the style in the context of 'mood creation'. If one takes the two orchestral pastoral pieces, the *Pastoral Rhapsody* and the *Paradise Rondel* (both entirely different from each other), it is the shape, impression and, most importantly, *mood* of the whole which is the overridingly important feature. Melody is important, but it is subservient to the overall intention of painting a large-canvas picture in which the atmosphere is dominant. Anyone who says that Howells could not write a tune has only to look at the *Chosen Tune*, the hymn tune *Michael*, and the later *Hymn to St Cecilia* to name but three examples to see that he was as capable as anyone in this direction: but it is just not the method by which he wanted to create these particular works. In this way, he has created a unique language which, like it or hate it, shows an ingeniously original mind taking a baton which has been handed on to him and running the next stretch of the race before handing it on again.

Whilst he was in the middle of these more highbrow thoughts he was 'being useful' in producing whole series of unison and two-part songs for use in schools. Marvellous songs like *The Wonderful Derby Ram*, *Holly Song*, *Four Horses* and *Sing Ivy* which were done more to earn a living than to enrich the art in any way, something which many composers did throughout this period. Each of these tiny miniatures nevertheless has something to offer which is certainly more than a technical exercise, and the lovely melodies created underline again Howells's ability in this way when it suited his needs.

Howells's diary throughout this period is a whirlwind of events and of meetings with all the top people of the day. Here is a typical short period: 15 February 1923: "Lunch with Scholes. See Vaughan Williams 3pm RCM"; 21 February: "Moeran to lunch at RCM 1pm. (Harold) Samuel's Bach Recital at RCM 4.45; 24th: "Holst wants me at Morley College"; 25 February: "Phantasy String Quartet South Place 6pm"; 27 February: "Sybil Eaton's recital"; 28 February: "Theatre and supper with A.C.B" (Boult); and so on. Moving in these circles and always in top gear it was not entirely surprising that, in due course, a commission should be forthcoming from the Royal Philharmonic Society for a *Piano Concerto* to be performed in the Queen's Hall in 1925.

The musical world was a-buzz with anticipation of a great musical occasion. Sargent was to conduct the work, making his debut with the Society: and Harold Samuel, famous for his Bach recitals, was to be the soloist. Things did not get off to a very auspicious start when Samuel received the score and disliked the work. Howard Ferguson, who was living in his house at the time, remembers being the 'orchestra' on a second piano for Samuel and recalls Samuel's attempts at getting the Society to release him from the engagement, which they refused to do.

On the day of the performance the hall was packed and was looking forward to a programme of music which included Vaughan Williams's *Pastoral Symphony*, Ireland's *Mai Dun*, and works by Bax and Lord Berners.

When Howells's *Concerto* came to an end the audience, as expected, burst into applause. Sir Thomas Armstrong remembers what followed: "I was sitting in the gallery, and Ralph Vaughan Williams not very far away from me. When the performance was over it was a sort of succès d'estíme and we applauded, and then some man stood up and shouted 'Well thank God that's over'; and immediately, of course, there was a reaction from Herbert's friends and we all stood up headed by Ralph Vaughan Williams and applauded strongly to counteract this display" (BBC/Green).

The man in question was a music critic called Robert Lorenz who was noted for his outspoken views. Howells remembered: "I wasn't surprised this man got up, but he got up for purely political reasons. You see there were cliques in those days, and he belonged very much to the Philip Heseltine clique who weren't at all friendly to the people I was working amidst, and I think was furious because I had been asked and commissioned to do this work instead of E.J. Moeran" (ibid).

Howells may have been able to be calm in reflection during that programme seventy or so years on, but at the time he was cut to the quick, and despite the fact that the work was at proof stage with the publishers he instantly withdrew it. Part of the problem was that, in all probability, Howells was sympathetic to the outburst. He had not found the work easy to write and the experimental form (similar to that used in his first *Violin Sonata*) of a single Sonata structure covering all three movements (first movement = exposition; second movement = development; third movement = recapitulation) relied heavily on sufficiently substantial melodic material to withstand the amount of repetition which would inevitably be required as part of the developmental process over a twenty-five minute span. The rather slight and jaunty first subject is insufficient for this purpose and leads the listener into the rather false impression of a light-weight work which, despite appearances, it is not. Howells's own pre-performance description of the piece called it "a diatonic affair, with deliberate tunes all the way – jolly in feeling, and attempting to get to the point as quickly as maybe" but this tells only part of the story.

First performances of new works are rather like giving birth: one's soul is laid bare and is subject to the minute scrutiny and the often ill-judged first impressions of critics and colleagues. In writing what he called a 'jolly' piece Howells was not being true to his natural creative nature which, as we have seen time and again, was at its most persuasive when creating 'mood' music in the manner of Vaughan Williams's *Pastoral Symphony*. Indeed, by far the most impressive part of this *Concerto* is the ruminative slow movement which has some truly beautiful music. Once again, though, one is left wishing that the eight-note theme were both more distinguished and more long-breathed – a most unusual criticism to be levelled at Howells who is usually attacked, especially by singers performing his later music, for phrases which are seemingly unending!

The reception of this *Concerto* was a defining moment in Howells's life. It was the first time that he taken a really serious knock, and the way in which he reacted proved that he was psychologically ill-equipped to cope with adverse criticism. This trait had been hinted at before (first *Piano Concerto*, second *Violin Sonata* etc) but had always been sufficiently overcome not to hinder the steady flow of composition. Now, he had what appeared to be a crisis of confidence and, for a while, simply dried up as a composer, writing only small-scale piano pieces, and revising earlier works. The only composition which could be said to be of any real significance in his output of the next six or seven years is *Lambert's Clavichord* written between 1926 and 1927 of which more in the next chapter. Ursula Howells, reflecting on this time, said: "The second *Piano Concerto* had a desperate effect on him. He was a mess, like so many people, underneath, and he wasn't big enough to overcome that" (UH/PS).

On 12 Monday April 1926 Howells noted in his diary: "Dear Sonnie born today at 4 p.m.". This was Michael Kendrick Howells. The Howells family was now complete and all were blissfully happy at the new arrival. Over the coming weeks he was shown off to admiring friends and acquaintances as various diary entries show: 27 April: "Sydney S[himmin] and Peggy to see baby", 28 April: "Finzi to see Dorothy and boy". On 2 May he notes that he "motored Adrian Boult to Chelmsford with Armstrong Gibbs and his wife, and motored to Thaxted, to see the astonishingly beautiful church". This must have been a revelation in more ways than just the appreciation of great church architecture. As Ursula remembers:

> Herbert was the world's worst driver. My mother always said that it was the only good turn that war did us – he gave up driving! Thank God, we persuaded him not to start up again afterwards. He was the sort of person who would be driving down

the right hand side of the road with something coming straight at us, saying 'get over onto your side!' He was always in the right, and everyone else would be wrong. I remember when we were up in Scotland and we were up above Glamis castle, he said 'look at that view!' and we were suddenly upside down in the ditch. The local farmer would then be called to get us out on a Sunday. He could just as well be turning a corner and put his foot on the accelerator rather than the brake. It was a nightmare!

(ibid)

What happened that May Sunday with Boult and Gibbs is not recorded.

Michael was christened on Sunday 23 May 1926 at 4 p.m. in Holy Trinity Church, Barnes by the Rev. Frank Inigo Harrison, after which the family settled down to their new existence with two growing children, an increasingly busy father, and a mother who was content to be at home and nurture them all. It all sounds serene and perfect, and at this stage in most respects it was. Domestic bliss was not to be the order of the day for long, however, as Howells's own magnetic attraction and his reciprocated penchant for attractive young ladies soon began to cause problems.

As Ursula Howells has pointed out:

The main trouble was that he and Dorothy were very fond of one another, but they should never have married. Mother had the most ghastly inferiority complex. She had a terrible childhood and upbringing. People are always going on about backgrounds now, but mother's was simply awful. She had no education and had a real complex about it. Father was, in a sense, an intellectual – a would-be academic. I could have seen Herbert perfectly happily being a don. They got on much better when they were older, but our childhood was one row after another.

I was amazed when I read what [Alan] Ridout said when I read it (1995) that "Herbert had married above his station". Absolute rubbish. Grandma [Dorothy's mother] was very beautiful and was having an affair with the local squire, and it is possible that the last two children, one of which was my mother, were the squire's. Her husband was very upset by her goings on and he committed suicide by holding his head down in a rain butt. Mother had either just been born, or was about to be born, so she never knew her father. By this time they had a pub in Deal in Kent, and her mother was drinking the profits away, and she fell down the stairs from top to bottom and broke her neck. Ten children were left. The only reason why mother might have been considered to be 'above' father was simply that some of the children were adopted by some very rich Americans and went over to the USA. Mother and her sister Bertha, however, were adopted by the local schoolmaster. That was the most ghastly set-up because Mrs Dawe, the foster mother, never consummated the marriage. Poor old Mr Dawe used to go to the pub on Friday nights and get blind drunk and then come back and knock her about, so Dorothy, mother and Bertha were always having to get between them. She and Bertha drew the short straw as all the others were very well placed. Uncle Walter even became a valet to King Edward VII.

(ibid)

Besides all this Ursula refers to an illegitimacy in the family

which, of course, in those days one didn't talk about and mother never ever did. It was Herbert who told me about it after it came to light when a cousin of mine went into the Foreign Office and it was discovered in their routine security checks. Dorothy's grandparents didn't marry, and so her father was illegitimate and was brought up with mother's name (Goozee), and while the rest of the family changed their name by deed poll to Ellinger, Mrs Dawe would never allow Aunt Bertha and Mother to change theirs. She was always known as Dawe, having been adopted by that family, but her real name was Goozee. She had a really dreadful young life. What saved her, Herbert said, was the most beautiful voice he had ever heard. In the end she was sent to London and was sent to a well-known singing teacher who, according to Herbert, wrecked many of the voices sent to her. Dorothy did a mixed bag of repertoire – ballads and so on – which father always thought was the lowest of the low. It always makes me laugh, as that's how they met!

Herbert was originally engaged to Kathleen Smale but broke it off when he met mother through her accompanist being ill and his being asked to stand in as pianist for one of her recitals. Kathleen Smale went on to marry a man called Kerr, and their daughter was Deborah Kerr. It was terribly funny when I was filming a lot at Ealing Studios; there were a lot of publicity shots and they asked me to come along and choose which ones I wanted. It was absolutely extraordinary because they did a

shoot of Deborah Kerr on the same day, and they muddled the two of us. It was only because I thought 'I haven't got blue eyes' that I recognised what had happened! Of course, we are not really so alike, but photographically it was extraordinary. I often wondered who had done what with whom!
(ibid)

Ursula's revelations about her mother's background when added to Herbert's own turbulent insecurities over his childhood deprivations add up to a heady brew of emotional repression. Howells also suffered all his life from depression; not clinical depression, but periods of depressed state of mind which could be brought on as much by a compositional block as by over-emotional involvement with his latest relationship. As Ursula remembers,

He got depressions. That, I think must be from his father. I remember as a child he would shut himself away usually because he couldn't succeed with a composition. He also had a great love-hate relationship with the College. There was always depression before the term started. 'Oh God, I've got to go back to that place'. Whether it was because he knew that he should have been spending more time composing or not, I don't know.
(ibid)

Through all these conflicting signals, however, life was going on apace. New and valuable work was being written – albeit in small quantities – and there was always the ever-present pleasure in his two talented and growing children – the stable background to his successful and burgeoning career.

SIX
Tragedy and Rebirth

In the mid-1920s Gerald Finzi was a regular visitor to the Howells household. The two families spent a whole month together at Mrs Champion's farm on Chosen Hill in the summer of 1925, and Robert Spearing recalls Howells telling him that he saw Finzi as an 'unofficial pupil' around this time. As Banfield points out (GF 63), Finzi most probably did not see it like this and he quotes Howells in conversation with Robert Spearing and artist Richard Walker (in April 1971), saying that

> Every alternate Sunday morning, he [Finzi] would turn up at my house, and the other Sundays in between he would turn up at either Ralph Vaughan Williams's house, in Dorking in those days, or at R.O. Morris's, in Chelsea; and he would pick our brains, quite legitimately; we'd discuss what he'd done, and sometimes we'd make suggestions, which ran counter to what he'd done perhaps. But we never any one of us knew that he ever took the slightest notice when we saw the finished work: we'd been put in our places!
> (CPC pp.364-5)

He also goes on to say:

> Although he would think he was the most modest man in the world, he had an enormous respect for being a composer; so that at home, I mean, it would be more than you'd dare to do to go

and interrupt him. If my wife wants to come into my room when I'm working and say 'beastly awful day' or something, she can do it. I should be greatly relieved that, for a moment, my mind has had a rest; but that wouldn't do for Gerald.

Ursula confirms this, but with the small caveat that if a radio was on downstairs or someone was singing in the house he would ask for quiet. She also tells a colourful story of the time when she was breeding budgerigars in an open-air cage at the bottom of the garden at 'Redmarley', a rented house in Station Road, Barnes, to which the family moved in 1928. These birds, of which there were some twenty-five, inevitably made a great deal of noise as they flew around. Howells used to love watching them, but found the noise intolerable when he was working. Padlocked as the cage was, Ursula came down to breakfast one morning to discover the door wide open and the birds all flown. She still does not know whether Herbert was responsible.

Having a brilliant father could be something of a liability, and Ursula felt that he wanted her to do everything almost the moment she could speak. She very much regrets that he took her to see Shakespeare when she was about four years old. This unfathomable experience remained with her throughout her acting career, as she never wanted to do Shakespeare. Howells also made her begin piano lessons before she could walk. Worse than this, however, was the fact that he decided to teach her. The same happened to Michael. Ursula remembers: "He taught me because I was his daughter. Piano lessons were a nightmare. Mother would sit downstairs in the sitting room waiting, and then Michael would have his. I would come downstairs in floods of tears every Sunday. Michael was much tougher. Whether or not he would have been musical I don't know. If I played the wrong note twice running, the heavens fell in! I always said later in life that he always expected me to come out of the womb able to play the Moonlight Sonata perfectly! He realised, in the end, that it was fatal to teach his own daughter, and I was sent to Dorothea Aspinall at the College. I couldn't bear the noises I made, and she said 'would you like me to get you out of it?'. She went to Herbert and got me off. I could always play by ear as a child, but he killed that, saying: 'you'll never learn to read music properly if you play by ear'." This was rich, coming from a man who spent so much time extemporising: the only instrument Ursula really wanted to play was the cello, but whether or not Howells felt that she should learn the piano first, or because he didn't want the expense of buying an instrument which might not be kept up, he would not allow it. His excuse was that Ursula would get bandy legs.

A great friend of Howells and the family was the harpsichord and clavichord maker Herbert Lambert of Bath. He was a multi-talented man who was also a remarkable photographer. He had been making a collection of portraits of leading British musicians, and this was how Howells met him. In a BBC broadcast in 1940 Howells recalled "In the summer of 1927 he lent me a clavichord – an entrancing instrument. I gave up a holiday, remaining in London with it. The only way to thank Lambert was to write a work for him. So I did *Lambert's Fireside* – actually written by Lambert's own fire-side on the hills outside Bath" (BBC 15 November 1940).

Howells went on to add a further eleven pieces to complete the set called *Lambert's Clavichord*. This is the first time that Howells so firmly nailed his 'Tudor reincarnation' colours to the mast. It is a remarkable set of pieces whose inspiration and model is obviously the Fitzwilliam Virginal Book and others of its type right down to the style of the dedicatory titles. Therefore the movements include such as *Fellowes Delight; de la Mare's Pavane; Sir Hugh's Galliard; My Lord Sandwich's Dreame* and so on. The final movement is a most telling (and dissonant) fugue which Howells has for himself *HH, His Fancy*.

Howells sent his friend Walter de la Mare a copy, being one of the dedicatees. De la Mare wrote to thank Howells, saying "It was a quite unexpected joy that awaited me inside the package, and I am off in a minute to Dick's room... with a forefinger poised for its first practice" (CPC p.418).

Sir Richard Terry (*The Queen*, 7 November 1928) wrote:

> Sooner or later it was bound to come that some modern English composer would set himself... to write music for these resusci-tated instruments of the past. The danger would be consider-able, had the first attempts been mere imitations of the old idiom.

Luckily the first attempt has been made by one whose creative musicianship cannot be called in question; whose sympathy with both the Tudor instruments and Tudor composers is undeniable, and above all it has been made by one who is content (out of the plenitude of his critical knowledge of Tudor music) to reproduce the spirit of the old music rather than to give us a mere reproduction of its mannerisms or a repetition of its clichés.

Mr Howells has absorbed all the wealth and variety of Tudor rhythms, but keeps his own individuality intact. His music is modern inasmuch as he uses chords and progressions unknown in Tudor times, but the *spirit* of the old composers is there all the while. In other words, he and his instruments are one.

(ibid p.419)

The utter honesty of these pieces and the sound world which they inhabit is in stark contrast to the failed *Piano Concerto* of such recent memory. Howells's rebuilding and rebirth really began with *Lambert's Clavichord*. We hear a new self-confidence, and an audible relief at being able to speak a language which is entirely his own, for nothing else like it existed in British music, as Terry hinted. Howells could plough his own entirely personal furrow without the fear of comparisons and reprisals. Here at last was a medium in which he could relax in the confidence that he had the technique, knowledge and 'intuitive affinity' with the composers of the period to make a kind of music which was absolutely his own. After this, Tudor-inspired music or musical forms featured often in his music. In its own way, *Lambert's Clavichord* was as much of a watershed in Howells's life as the second *Piano Concerto*, but unlike the latter was entirely a force for positive good, showing him a path which he could follow, being true to his roots and faithful to Vaughan Williams's example.

The year 1931 saw Howells awarded the first John Collard Fellowship, an award held for three years and worth some £300 a year to the recipient. It was an award made to a distinguished musician in the fields of composition, research or performance. In being the first such award holder Howells was marked out as being among the principal musicians of the day. Nearly twenty years later in 1959 he was further honoured by being made the third John

Collard Life Fellow following Elgar and Vaughan Williams.

Despite the stated significance of *Lambert's Clavichord* it is important not to paint a picture of such a 'road to Damascus' conversion that all his music after this date became miniaturist and Tudor-inspired. Nothing could be further from the truth, as demonstrated by the second *Organ Sonata*, written in 1932.

The *Sonata* was written for George Thalben-Ball, contemporary and friend, who had played the organ for Howells's wedding. He was acknowledged as one of the great virtuoso organists of the century. The *Sonata's* first performance was given at the Royal Albert Hall in May 1934. The London Contemporary Music Centre combined with the Organ Music Society to promote a concert of works by Conrad Beck, Sibelius, Kaminsky, Roussel, Jarnach, Honneger, Milhaud, Vierne, Tournemire and Howells. Howells's *Sonata* was given by far the lion's share of space in the programme for the event, and the work attracted a great deal of interest. Arthur Milner writing in the *Musical Times* much later in 1964 said of it: "One of the striking things about the Sonata is that it is not merely fine *organ* music: it is fine music in its own right, irrespective of medium. There are comparatively few organ sonatas of which this could be said.... This is musician's music, in the best sense of the term, to which one goes back again and again with increasing satisfaction" (MT 12.64).

The *Sonata* is a big-scale work in three movements which makes severe demands of the player. It is very tightly organised, and the thematic development complex and absorbing. One fragment of melody worth highlighting appears almost as a leitmotif throughout Howells's music for the rest of his life, and the most well-known example of it is the opening bar of the *Gloria* to the *Collegium Regale* evening canticles:

Howells uses this fragment repeatedly, although when asked by the present author if he attached any significance to it, given the frequency of its use, he could not think of any, and it felt as if he had not really been aware of it.

Harvey Grace, writing a penetrating review of the work for the *Musical Times* in April 1934, noted that "It is commonplace that works worth knowing are apt to hold one off at the outset. That is my experience with this Sonata. A first reading merely raised doubts, but fuller acquaintance leaves me with a conviction that we have here a composition of outstanding quality" (MT 4.34).

Very few organists since then have taken the work up. It may be possible to justify this on the grounds of its technical demands, and the fact that it requires an instrument of cathedral-size resources to do it justice. Perhaps more to the point, though, it requires a real sympathy with Howells's intentions. Anyone opening the score and hoping for another *Rhapsody* or *Psalm Prelude* will no doubt be disappointed, and they may well be perplexed. They will find a work of no small degree of aggression, of obviously serious intent and, being absolute music, with no helpful text or programmatic element to help the imagination. This is why Arthur Milner called it "musicians' music" (MT 12.64). The work is startlingly original (as, to a greater or lesser degree are all Howells's organ works in the context of the period) and completely breaks the mould of existing organ sonatas from whichever corner of the globe they may come.

The other major work which was written in the same year as that first performance (1933) was the *Kent Yeoman's Wooing Song*. It was written as a wedding present for Keith and Cristabel Falkner. Both had been students at the RCM in the 1920s when Howells was a young professor and they became life-long friends. Falkner eventually became Director of the RCM when Howells was Senior Professor. At this stage, the work was only completed in short score and had to wait until a performance in the Proms on 10 September 1953 before Howells orchestrated it. When it was heard on that occasion the attitude of the critics was summed up by Felix Aprahamian: "It was noted that the appearance of this work might have been taken to mark a new and admirable step towards a more urgent and concentrated style of writing, but for the fact that this secular cantata had been attributed previously to 1933" (PH p.100).

This "more urgent and concentrated style" was rather comically described by Christopher Palmer as his 'Country-and-Western style' (CPC p.192). It is perfectly true that the swashbuckling swagger of this music represents Howells in what might be thought of as 'lusty milkmaid' mode, swapping heady distant views of the Malverns for more earthy concerns. In reflection of the amalgamated text from Vautor and Ravenscroft the music of the outer movements is also genuinely humorous – a mood rarely encountered in Howells's work – while the central movement is Howells in his most romantically charged mode. The music of this middle movement shows Howells displaying his true colours and, rarely too, wearing his heart on his sleeve. It is easy to see why Hilary Macnamara, contributing to a BBC broadcast at the time of Howells's centenary, described him as "possibly the most passionate individual I have ever met – amazingly passionate about just about every aspect of life" (BBC/Green). Howells at his most passionate in music is Howells at his most persuasive, for, like the clavichord pieces at the other end of the spectrum, he is here at his most natural and unaffected. Christopher Palmer asks "is there a more ardent love-song in English music?" (CPC p.192) and surely the answer has to be 'no'. The final plagal cadence of this movement is what really seals the knot. It is a wonderful moment. Palmer also quotes a letter which Ernest Bradbury wrote to Howells on the subject of cadences which is worth repeating in this context:

> As I write... the strains of Ralph's Pavane float up to me from the drawing room. It is Nick [Ernest's son], not a natural keyboard player... wrestling with, caressing those chords and harmonies. He's just cottoned on: this lovely, rare world of shifting musical lights and gracious harmonies, the splendour and grace and beauty of it all; and, to me, hiding my feelings, it all seems too unspeakably lovely, so grand and *permanent*.
>
> He points to the thrill of the closing bars, and I tell him he is wrong – and draw his attention to the last four bars of *Finzi's Rest*... adding that from Tudor times our composers have always been in the front rank in the matter of cadences.... I thank God for a lot of Howells in a pretty damned world.
>
> (CPC pp.192-3n)

The *Kent Yeoman's Wooing Song* demands light-hearted treatment and is an ideal (and heartfelt) wedding present in its subject matter. It concerns a rather boorish Yeoman's son from Kent who finds the girl he wants but then proceeds to list all the reasons why he "cannot come every day to woo". If she is not able to cope with this she will miss the opportunity as "he'll seek some otherwhere". In the other poem 'Mother, I will have a husband (Vautor)', we find the girl desperate for a partner ("Mother, I will have a husband, and I will have him out of hand!") and willing to have almost anything presumably to assuage her passion and, one rather suspects, to get away from said mother! The serious wooing, as we have seen, is done in the slow movement; and all parts come together in a riotous finale. This is enacted on three simultaneous levels – soprano and baritone soloists, and chorus including one level at 3/2 and another at 2/2. It is a true bacchanale. At the end, the soprano soloist audibly flings herself at her man by lunging for a long-held top C underneath which the whole riot is brought to a lusty conclusion.

Reviewing the work in the *Musical Times* after its first performance in 1953 Martin Cooper reflects that "It is good humour which characterises this music of Howells, not the fictitious merriment of an imaginary 'merry England' but that warm and earthy sanity which is the true terrestrial counterpart of that celestial other-worldliness which breathes from the same composer's *Hymnus Paradisi*" (PH p.102).

In 1934, Howells was commissioned to write a work for the Belle Vue National Brass Band Contest held in Manchester. The result was a Suite he called *Pageantry* and it is yet another work which encourages reflection on the huge variety in Howells's output. He writes absolutely to the manner born as if he were a northerner by spirit and temperament with the sound of the Salvation Army Band in his veins. A contemporary appraisal in *The British Bandsman* is warm in its praise: "I do not think anything finer than this has been done for the brass band; it has many great merits, but the greatest is the splendid scope which it provides for the imagination. Our great bands will revel in it, and the smaller ones will wish to try it after, once they have heard it". John Russell and J.H. Elliot writing about 'The Brass Band Movement' singled it out as "the outstanding work derived from Belle Vue", which had had music from Bantock, Elgar, Holst and Ireland (PH p.150).

All this highly successful activity on the composition front was most welcome after the debacle of the second *Piano Concerto*. Howells had worked his way through the self-inflicted block and was now producing works of self-evident quality even if his teaching and other professional commitments prevented him from spending as much time writing as he (and others) would have liked. Life was proceeding apace, and a list of his adjudicating and examining commitments for one year alone (1933) reads like an A-Z map of Britain: Darlington, Dursley, Dorking, London Co-op, Lewes, Amersham, Reigate, Northampton, Arbroath, Stafford, Bedford, Norwich, Maidstone, Lytham, Devizes, Leamington, Enfield, Woking, Stratford, Wadebridge, Chelmsford and Blackpool. There was a subtext to all this time spent away from home, however, and a real clue is given in his 1934 diary. Inside the front cover appears the inscription: "HNH Marlborough Downs 1.5.34". This is not in Howells's handwriting. Then, on 1 May, when he is examining or adjudicating in Devizes, the following entry has been made by Howells: "This book mine. A great and lovely day in Wiltshire. V. in excelsis". The following day we read: "Cottley. Devizes. V. in excelsissimo".

This weakly coded language refers to Valerie Trimble, Howells's current mistress, who had gone up to Devizes to join him for what were obviously two passionate days. It is probable that she gave him the diary, as there are no entries before 1 May, and few afterwards, and this explains the front cover inscription. The likelihood is that she did not want these special days to be forgotten despite the obvious risks of an easily broken code.

Throughout his life and well into old age Howells had a succession of girlfriends. His daughter Ursula is absolutely candid about it: "Herbert was ruled by sex. He was unbelievably attractive to the female sex and was just as attracted to them" (UH/PS).

She also vividly remembers Howells bringing his girlfriends for her to 'vet'. This seemed very important to him, even though a disconcerting role for a daughter to play when her mother was sitting blithely at home. Ursula continued: "After a lot of guilt and soul-searching I realised that as long as Mother didn't know what was going on, the extra-marital relations helped to keep the marriage together. His fondness and concern for Mother never wavered. This was the only way I could temper my own loyalties" (ibid).

And so the relationships went on. Ursula was always amazed at the length of time they lasted, sometimes "year on year". "He always got desperately emotionally involved which also counted a lot for the depressions. He used to ring me up when I was on tour anywhere and ask if I could meet him and the current girlfriend" (ibid).

However, other quite different events were in store. On 12 April in both 1932 and 1933 there are penned entries in the diaries recording Michael's birthday: "Darling Mick is 6 years old today"; and in 1933 "Beloved Mick is 7 today". Little did Herbert or Dorothy realise what was ahead when those happy days were celebrated.

In 1932 Howells wrote an unaccompanied *Requiem*. The discovery of the date of composition of this music (in a letter quoted below) turned upside-down the popularly held notion that Howells wrote it directly in response to his son's death. Howells even said that Michael had added a note to the score about a week before his death, and ringed the note in question on the page which is now in the RCM Library. All this shows that the *Requiem* was already an ongoing 'project' at this time. In a letter dated 13 October 1932 and addressed to Diana Oldridge, Howells said that "It's done specially for King's College Cambridge – otherwise I might not have dreamed of it" (CPC p.98). In fact Howells never sent it to King's, and there is no record of any performances.

In Howells's output the *Requiem* is in a direct line of succession from the very early double choir setting of *Even such is time* written as "student homework for Dr Wood" which we came across in Chapter 2, and *Blessed are the dead*, another double choir work written in 1920 in memory of his father and for some reason left incomplete (although it has now been most successfully completed by Patrick Russill). Howells may have declared in his letter to Diana Oldridge that "I *didn't* write it [the *Requiem*] on my technique", but he certainly wrote it as a result both of techniques learnt with Charles Wood, and in his very extensive exposure to Elizabethan choral music and its counterparts elsewhere in Europe. The *Requiem* has the heady mixture of Palestrina's purity of expression coupled to a subterranean white-hot lava. The effect is extraordinary.

It is something of a mystery that he did not send it to King's when first completed, but that he did not do so was an act of grace given the tragic turn of events in 1935 which would bring it sharply into focus so soon.

The summer of that fateful year began full of hope and happiness. The whole family visited the Finzis at their house on Downshire Hill in Hampstead. Joy Finzi had just given birth to her first son, Christopher, on 12 July. Afterwards the Howells family went for a ramble on Hampstead Heath which Howells later noted as "Mick's only sight of it". All the small boy pleasures of that time were given full rein: a much-treasured visit to the Oval to see Nottingham play Surrey with Larwood batting, and time spent in the garden at home making a triple signal for his model railway.

On 9 August the family left for their summer holiday. Never much interested in more exotic places, the lure of Gloucestershire was as strong as ever. They stayed at a farmhouse in Bream in beautiful countryside close to Lydney. It was a perfect location, especially for the children who could explore woods and country lanes, watch cows being milked, and generally inhale the magic of country life. They walked, cycled, visited family locally and even went to Cheltenham to see Hammond make a century in a county match against Middlesex. Michael, a keen sportsman, was also given a cricket lesson whilst in Cheltenham. The line in Matthew Arnold's poem 'A Scholar Gipsy' which evokes "All the live murmur of a summer's day" seems to describe the hum of the whole family's pleasure as it relaxed away from London.

Then suddenly, everything changed. In one of two diaries Howells kept at this time he noted that during the course of a walk from Bream back to Noxon Farm Mick "seemed lack-lustre and complained of feeling a little sick. I feared the distance for M if we went all round the roads. So I... found a short cut to the left which took us over a winding route past open ground, then through a wood – still damp and slippery with recent rains (M fell once) – that led us to the back barns of Noxon Farm. We paused by the pond, watching about a dozen fishermen angling for carp."

With plenty to do, and no other signs of any illness, Michael stayed on the farm all the next day while Herbert and Dorothy visited uncle Alfred in Lydney. On their way back, however, they had a

1. Lydney High Street

2. Oliver Howells (Howells's father)

3. Elizabeth Howells (Howells's mother)

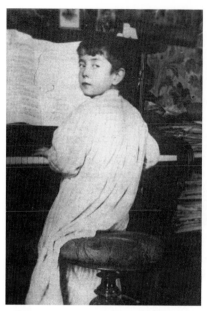

4. Howells at the piano aged about five

5. Howells in 1907 aged fourteen

6. Howells at Salisbury in March 1917 (aged twenty-four)

7. "Taken in the sitting room I used at the Choristers' School, Salisbury." Howells aged about twenty-six.

8. Florence (Florrie) Howells: Howells's sister who taught him the piano

9. Dorothy Howells (Howells's wife) in about 1920

10. Family photograph of Howells with Michael and Ursula

11. Michael (back row, far left) in his cricket team at Colet Court School

12. Michael

13. Michael

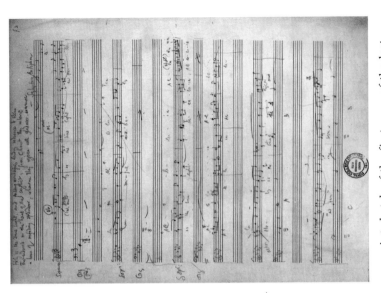

15. The manuscript sketch of the first page of the last movement of *Hymnus Paradisi* with the text suggested by Sir Thomas Armstrong

14. Michael's grave at Twigworth

16. Ursula

17. 'Uncle Ralph' with Howells,
Gloucester 1956

18. Ivor Gurney

19. Herbert Sumsion, Worcester
1957

20. Harold Darke with Howells,
Worcester 1951

21. Recording *Hymnus Paradisi* in 1970: Heather Harper (seated), producer Ronald Kinlock Anderson, Sir David Willcocks (holding score), Howells, and Robert Tear just behind him.

22. Sir Adrian Boult with Howells at the recording of the *Concerto for Strings* in 1974. (Howells died the day after Boult)

strange experience which was later seen as some kind of foreboding:
"a forbidding evening... getting back to Bream by bus D and I
turned left up the lane opp. the church, (to arrive *later* in the house)
and all the way, bats flew about our heads, and this worried D
deeply for some strange reason. Somehow I hated the eerie nature
of that walk from the bus to the farm. And I know D did."

On Tuesday 3 September Michael busied himself mowing lawns
after which the family went to Lydney for tea with Grace Jarratt (sister of Maurice Jarratt). On the way home Michael complained of
being unwell and was sent to bed early. From this point events accel-
erated with alarming speed, and Howells's diary conveys the nature
of the unfolding drama with chilling brevity:

> Wednesday 4: Mick's coming to our room in early morning.
> Temperature. Bad back. Dr Nanda sent for. Herbert
> arrived with coat he thought Mick had lost. Dr N came at
> 2.30. Chill?
> To St. B[riavels] for medicine. At 9 o'clock in Taylor's car.
> Thursday 5: Mick worse. Dr N at 11.15. Orders for London.
> Ambulance and Cheltenham Flier – London – Dr
> Dowling. Nursing Home. Dr Hunt. Fearful anxiety.
> Friday 6: Nursing home at 8.45 – Dr H at 9am. With M most
> of the morning – lunch with Scotts. M again at 2.30. Grave
> change. Mrs Fisher came – Mick worse always. Dr H 7pm.
> Hope, then despair. Dr Brunton. Dr Fisher... Mick died at
> 10.10pm. +

Howells always said that he never forgot the "luridly spectacu-
lar" sunset over Gloucestershire that night as they drove away from
the Forest of Dean to Gloucester Station to get the boy back to
London. Ursula remembers Michael turning 'bluey-black' as his
lungs ceased to function properly. In fact he had the most virulent
form of polio. Ursula made the point that "it was lucky in one way
that there was only one iron lung in London, and it was on the other
side of London. It would have been possible to get it to him, but the
doctors felt that it might be kinder to let him die given that he would
anyway be totally paralysed for the rest of what would have been a
much shortened life. So they had this awful decision to make, but
fortunately he died while they were deliberating."

There is some relief in the practical things which have to be put into motion following a death. So Howells went with Dr Fisher to deal with the death certificate and arranged for Michael to be taken home to 'Redmarley'. The boy arrived at 11 p.m. "to rest in his own room" as Howells touchingly put it.

The next day members of the Howells family began to arrive, and Arthur Benjamin called in the afternoon. Having looked at Gloucester Cemetery and hated it, arrangements had been made with Canon Cheesman to have Michael buried at Twigworth where Herbert and Dorothy had married, and where Ivor Gurney was to be buried just two years later.

Wednesday 11 September: "They came for Mick at 8.30 a.m., and we watched him set out for Gloucestershire and Peace. Agony by road through Oxfordshire and over the Cotswolds. We followed by 10.45 train from Paddington, and went straight to Twigworth: and so took gentle leave of him."

And so ended the terrible saga, begun so full of hope as a happy family holiday back in their native Gloucestershire. They took comfort from the warmth of their close friends, but both parents were inconsolable. Howells wrote to Diana Oldridge a few days later saying "I feel too frozen to write – at any rate yet – I wish I could comfort D – Keep us in mind for a long time. And if you're driving past Twigworth, go and greet what was Mick".

Ursula remembers the period immediately post-Michael's death. "Herbert was an extremely emotional person. I don't know what he was like religiously before Michael's death, but afterwards, every weekend we went to Gloucester [from London to Twigworth]. We used to live in church. But that was an emotional thing as Michael was buried there. As far as religion goes I think he adored the music and the buildings – he adored cathedrals. Emotionally, he had a sort of spiritual sense. I know he said to me, about a year before he died when we were sitting one day in the dining room: 'I don't believe there's anything'. I was very surprised that he said it as definitely as that. That was the only surprise I had. Not that he didn't believe. It was the fact that he said it, and come out with it" (UH/PS).

Howells's diary for 1936 shows just how much time was spent at Twigworth after Michael's death. Christmas 1935 was spent with the

Sumsions at Gloucester (20 College Green) "to be near Michael's resting place". This was an act of supreme friendship on the part of the Sumsions, whose Christmas must have been put under a pretty severe cloud by the deeply mourning Howells family. The good news was that Howells had begun to put pen to paper once more, and on 2 January he worked on the de la Mare setting *The Lady Caroline*. There is a sense, however, that it is a very half-hearted attempt at occupation. Everything conjured ghosts for the family, and most especially a walk on Minchinhampton Common the following day which "blanketed in shifting fog" was "cold and inhospitable".

Each day also brought its ritual visit to Twigworth until 11 January when Howells wrote:

> Every visit to Mick is a 'hail and farewell!' This morning, in weather swept clean and blue and of miraculous visibility, D and I went alone. The sense of rains and saturation depressed us... and the coming away was the harder because today we would be leaving him in beloved Gloucestershire, and going ourselves back to London, where,... apart from Barnes which he knew and loved... there is no consolation for us. From now on Gloucestershire matters even more than it ever did – and with hearts there (with Mick and the places most beloved) the 'Cheltenham Flier' was a sort of spiritual-murder-on-wheels for at least 3 people in it today.

Later, there was a further twist in the story. It is surprising to see Howells describing Michael "as (only) finally (laid) to rest" a year later (11 September 1936), rather than when he was first buried. This was because Michael had originally been buried in a plot well to the east of the church. Twigworth's ground is notoriously marshy and often floods, and the Howells had been constantly worried by Michael's grave filling with water. In a further dedication at the new graveside "Canon Cheesman read brief and lovely prayers – Dorothy and I, and just Mr Pitt of Gloucester – and sun and pale light and quiet skies and trees and a few birds and fresh flowers... and I think we at last felt less desolate than for the whole of the past year."

Eric Smith, a native of Twigworth who still lives in Longford, the next door village, was a chorister and, for some while, acting organist at the church. He was twenty-six at the time of Michael's death and remembers all too well the terrible problems of water-logging in the churchyard. He recalls as a choirboy being called to sing for a funeral and Canon Cheesman instructing the boys to leave at once when it was over. Needless to say they did not obey him and they all rushed out to the grave where they saw that during the course of the service the water had risen right up. Boys being boys they took to rocking the floating coffin 'like a boat'. It is no wonder that the Howells wanted to move Michael to a drier spot at the north west of the church. No wonder, then, that when he had been moved, they felt that the boy was finally 'at rest'. Eric Smith recalls that the larger grave surround was built later to accommodate the whole family (ES/PS).

In writing the letter to Diana Oldridge, already quoted, a few days after Michael's death when Howells indicated that he was "too frozen to write", the pain is palpable. Too often, though for entirely understandable reasons, Dorothy and Ursula are overlooked in this grieving process, and all eyes are focused on Howells himself, because of what followed. Ursula points out, however, that it was Dorothy who nearly had a nervous breakdown. In some ways, Howells was the fortunate member of this small family unit: he could immerse himself in work, he could get out and meet lots of friends and colleagues; and above all and most importantly, he alone had the ability to assuage his grief through the cathartic process of writing music. Neither Dorothy nor Ursula were able to channel their grief in this way.

Ironically, too, it was Ursula, as young as she was, and seeing her inconsolable father, who suggested that he should write about Michael in music. And thus it was that *Hymnus Paradisi* made its first uncertain steps towards the towering achievement which a Gloucester audience eventually witnessed for the first time fifteen years later, one day after the anniversary of Michael's death, on 7 September 1950.

The story of *Hymnus Paradisi* is a complex one. Howells was extremely well read, and apart from his natural interest in books nurtured by his father when he was a boy, he had spent hours and even days at a time discussing all aspects of literature with Ivor Gurney. It was therefore not surprising that he came across Helen Waddell's book about early medieval literature and learning *The Wandering Scholars* and its sequel *Medieval Latin Lyrics* (translations of the scholars' work). Helen Waddell's work was to exert a powerful influence over Howells, and that it did so should come as little surprise to anyone who has read her matchless translations which her biographer Dame Felicitas Corrigan has said, 'turned poetry into poetry'. The fact that she was Irish and therefore also a Celt has enormous bearing on the synergy between these two great creative artists. Waddell's extraordinary command of language was only part of her gift; we would compare that with Howells's command of musical technique. Waddell's real genius was in creating new out of old, getting under the skin of the early medieval poem and re-creating it as if it were hers, in her own language. This is the exact equivalent of what Vaughan Williams had done with his *Tallis Fantasia* and what Howells did with his *Lambert's Clavichord* and other similarly inspired works. Felicitas Corrigan's preface to the *Songs of the Wandering Scholars* begins with a quotation from Helen Waddell's writings: "The scholar's lyric of the twelfth century seems as new a miracle as the first crocus: but its earth is the leafdrift of centuries of forgotten scholarship". Corrigan goes on to say: "The beauty of that image clad in its exquisite language falls gratefully on ears besieged by a contemporary clamour for agrochemicals, pharmaceuticals and chemical intermediates. Ecology applies to literature as well as to life; indeed, they may be synonyms. And before it is too late, we need to recall the incontrovertible truth that underlines all Helen Waddell's work – that our Western civilisation is firmly rooted not only in the Christian faith, but also in the immemorial Latin tongue of the classical poets. Both faith and language are being deliberately jettisoned today" (SWS p.7).

Howells discovered Prudentius's *Hymnus circa exsequias defuncti* in Waddell's *Medieval Latin Lyrics* and made a setting which, like the double choir motet in memory of his father, remained incomplete. But little did he realise just how important 'nunc suscipe, terra, favendum, gremioque hunc concipe molli' was to be to *Hymnus Paradisi*. It was equally central, much later in his life, to the *Motet on the Death of President Kennedy* which actually used Waddell's translation of the Latin just quoted: "Take him, earth, for cherishing, / To thy tender breast receive him". In the event, neither the poem nor the setting was used in *Hymnus*, although the Latin title was used as a subtitle to the whole work. One could say that it pervades the work as, in a sense, it was its genesis.

The *Requiem* completed, as if by some terrible prescience so soon before Michael's death, was extensively used, and formed the basis of the new work whilst retaining its own identity and integrity. It underwent a complete metamorphosis, however, when translated into the large forces of orchestra, solo soprano and tenor, and chorus. Christopher Palmer, who conducted definitive research into the origins and various stages of composition of *Hymnus Paradisi*, produced fascinating charts in his Centenary Celebration tribute to Howells (CPC p.101). The reader who wants to discover the minutiae of Howells's approach to writing the work must refer to the chapter devoted to it in that book. It is not the place in this narrative to discuss the work in such detail. There are, however, some points which are worthy of mention here. First, that Palmer points out that it is likely that the *Kyrie* which eventually became the first movement of the *Missa Sabrinensis* was originally intended for *Hymnus*, and that this is supported by the fact that in its original version it is scored for only two soloists rather than the four which *Missa Sabrinensis* requires. Second, work on *Hymnus* was started earlier than might have been supposed especially in the light of Howells's 'frozen' remarks.

Given Howells's religious feelings (as stated by his daughter above), and his feelings of utter devastation through this period (he realised that he was becoming an 'utter bore' to his friends) the principal theme of 'light' – 'Et lux perpetua luceat eis' pervading *Hymnus Paradisi* is all the more remarkable. It is therefore not especially surprising that Howells had difficulty in finding a suitable text for the final movement of the work.

Sir Thomas Armstrong remembered how he (Armstrong) came to find the missing link.

> He didn't want it to end with sadness and tragedy but with hope, and this is why he found it difficult to select a text for the

last movement. Just at that time I happened to be reading an anthology by Robert Bridges called 'A Testament of Beauty' [as he remembered it, but actually 'The Spirit of Man'] and this extract was quoted by Robert Bridges and was in my mind; and I drew his attention to it. He said "that is exactly what I'm looking for". It starts: "Holy is the true light and passing wonderful, lending radiance to them that endure in the heat of the conflict".
(BBC / Green)

This great apotheosis was begun remarkably soon, and in Howells's diary entry two days after "Mick's 10th birthday" is noted on 12 April 1936 (Easter Day that year), he writes: "Shopping: then working at 'Holy is the true light'. Twigworth & back in the afternoon. Work again 6-8". He notes 'work' for the following three days, and then on Saturday 18th: "A rugger match at Kingsholm: with young John and Peter Sumsion – and Ursula. A brilliant and exciting sunset." He also notes, with understandable ruefulness: "The first Rugger match seen by the 2 Sumsion boys". Finding son-substitutes became a feature of his life, not in a morbid way, but with a kind of fascination which a bereaved father might compare the stages his own son might have passed through to those of others. Robert Spearing points to Hilary Macnamara's elder son Peter as one very important example in Howells's life.

It is very moving to read the continuing diary entries which point to his distressed state of mind. The following week he is almost living in Twigworth as well as working on the "revised Requiem". When the time comes for him to return to London once again, he notes: (27 April 1936) "Twigworth... London on 'Cheltenham Flier'. Heartache".

Nevertheless life had to be lived, and his return to London saw the return of a full timetable and the outward appearance of the trappings of normality. On 13 June, a new challenge and opportunity was presented when he was offered the post of Director of Music at St Paul's Girls' School in succession to Gustav Holst. Holst had died in 1934 and Vaughan Williams had taken over in the interregnum period of two years whilst the school authorities deliberated over a possible successor. In the end it was RVW who wrote to Howells persuading him to take it on. In accepting the position, Howells knew that his duties would not be onerous. He had a small amount of departmental administration, and in addition, conducted the senior orchestra, choir and class singers and was responsible for putting on concerts. These days it would be regarded almost as a sinecure, but for St Paul's their prestigious heads of music were what helped give their school the edge over the competition such as it was. Howells stayed as Director of Music until 1962, a remarkable tenure by any standards.

As a postscript to this terrible period, it is haunting to see an entry in his diary as a memorandum at the end of the week of 4 October 1936 in which he says: "During the night of Monday and Tues. I dreamed of Mick. He sat on my knee, looking well and happy, and was quietly affectionate. He said 'I am not really gone from you. I am with you always'."

SEVEN
Commemorations and Music: 'In Time of War'

The year 1937 dawned on a Friday and found the Howells family once again in Gloucester and visiting Twigworth and going walking with Ursula on Wainload's Hill. They were back at Twigworth the next day, and on the following day (Sunday) for Matins, Herbert returning for the 6.30 p.m. service by himself. After that, it was business as usual: catching the early morning train to London on 4 January, and attending a 'motor case' at the quarterly sessions in Oxford on the fifth. There are no details about this, but he was an appalling driver, as has already been noted, and it is likely that he had been involved in a minor mishap involving a court appearance. Term began at the RCM on the sixth, and so the normal pattern of life resumed.

His diary indicates how much of a *multum in parvo* lifestyle he was leading at this time. He had to balance his near full-time schedule at the RCM with his teaching commitments at St Paul's Girls' School; his examining and adjudicating all over the country; an increasing amount of broadcasting for the BBC; and, let's not forget, his compositional work. It appears that he only attended St Paul's Girls' School on Mondays (it is likely that it was more than this in reality), and that even on those days he spent two-and-a-half hours in the middle of the day at the RCM, returning to Brook Green at 1.45 p.m. and staying until 6.45 p.m. Ursula was by now fourteen years old and was a pupil at the school. On 18 March she was confirmed in St Paul's Cathedral, two days after Howells had noted "Minx's first trip to RCM", his nickname for her.

Howells's presence at St Paul's Girls' School was causing adolescent hearts to flutter. Ursula remembers that "life was hell for me at school because the girls all fell madly in love with him and I was given notes to take home to him. And when they were either never delivered or answered, I was just not spoken to. It was quite extraordinary". She goes on to underline the point made in the last chapter: "This was the trouble; he had this enormous attraction for women. He had it very easy, didn't he? I mean, *too easy*" (UH/PS).

Well, in one sense he 'had it too easy', but in another, inevitable problems arose because of it. One of the potentially most hazardous of all reached its climax on Thursday 27 May 1937 when he noted quite simply in his diary "V's natality". Ursula remembers that "Father was in a most terrible state because Valerie Trimble had *said* she was pregnant, and so Herbert had had to tell mother about it. When we were alone in the sitting room he said 'come and sit down. I am going to talk to mother'; and he went on to say that I was going to go to friends for the day. It was so odd knowing perfectly well what was going on and having to pretend that I didn't. I thought 'well, this is going to be the end of the marriage'. It was about nine o'clock that evening when they rang up to say that I was to come home, but somehow things seemed to have been patched up" (UH/PS). It turned out that Valerie was not pregnant after all. Whether, in the classic way, this was her attempt to stake a claim over Howells, or whether she really thought she was pregnant, is the subject of conjecture. It is nevertheless interesting that despite his turbulent emotional state over the loss of Michael, he apparently felt unable to stop these extra-marital liaisons, although he was often racked by guilt. The need, however, was stronger than the resolution to stop it, and his sex drive was the inner motor which kept his creative life humming.

In August he took the family to Scotland for the summer holiday, glorying in the sights and scenery. The twentieth was a "radiant day – into Arbroath town: then on to cliffs with D, Ursula and Tommy (son of the friends with whom they were staying) – Rocks, sun, motor boat and bees nest". He also worked a great deal on his submissions for his Oxford D.Mus examination which he was to sit in the autumn in order to become an examiner for that degree himself. The works he was to submit were the *Fantasia* for cello and orchestra; the small orchestra version of the song cycle *In Green Ways*; and an essay, 'Precursors of the Mass'. He also submitted the score of his *Piano Quartet* for good measure.

In the meantime, the Three Choirs Festival was coming up, this year at Gloucester. The day after returning to London from Scotland he was at the RCM rehearsing his *Elegy* for performance the following week in the festival. As if to dedicate himself he went at once to Twigworth, returning the next day (Sunday) for the morning service, before attending the opening service of the festival in the cathedral in the early afternoon. The *Elegy* was included in the Thursday evening concert together with Kodály's *Te Deum* and Verdi's *Requiem*.

Later that month, on the twenty-fifth, the Howells family were at the Alexandra Palace for the National Brass Band Championships. Howells's *Pageantry*, which had scored such a singular success in the year of its premiere (1934), was once again the test piece for all the contesting bands. This time it was the Foden's Band which carried away the laurels.

The process through which Howells passed to take his D.Mus at Oxford took place on 23 and 24 November. Christopher Palmer passed it off in his 'Centenary Celebration' saying: "At this stage in Howells's career the 'examination' aspect of the procedure could be little more than a formality, and consisted basically of his chatting to Sir Hugh Allen and Dr Sydney Watson!" (CPC p.85). In fact, John Williams, who was a close friend of Howells from the time when he was a choral scholar at St John's College, Cambridge and Howells was acting organist, states that Howells took the examination extremely seriously, and took a great deal of trouble over it. This even extended to taking lessons from H.K. Andrews, a former pupil, who was then organist at New College.

No doubt there was pleasant, civilised discussion between the principal protagonists in the process, but an Oxford D.Mus is no light-hearted matter whoever you are, and the award will have been based on real and rigorous assessment. Given Howells's own respect for learning, he will have been under no illusion as to the seriousness or status of the degree which he was attempting to attain. Oddly, he was back in Oxford again the following week as an examiner for the Associated Board. He must have felt the irony of the differing requirements and standards of the two types of examination as his own scholarly fate was being decided behind the closed doors of the Music Faculty down the road. Success was, in reality, assured, and he returned to the city on 11 December to receive his degree. He was already a member of Queen's College, having taken the B.Mus degree (for which he submitted the ballad *Sir Patrick Spens*) in 1934.

The new work submitted for this examination was the cello *Fantasia*. This big-scale one-movement work was written between 1936 and 1937 and, along with *Hymnus Paradisi*, was the first major work to follow Michael's death. It is not quite as simple as that, however, as Howells had been writing a *Cello Concerto* from about 1933. He completed two movements but only made rough sketches of the third. It was a project which seemed endlessly to fascinate him, as he kept returning to it for many years to come but he never completed it. The *Fantasia* is a reworking of the first movement. There is a danger that incorrect assumptions may be made due to the date of the writing of the *Fantasia* (as opposed to the first movement of the *Concerto*) and its elegiac nature. As with *Hymnus*, where the *Requiem* which provided much of the musical material had *pre-ceded* Michael's death, so with this *Fantasia*. Begun and possibly completed in its original version before September 1935 when Michael died, it was only brought out to serve its new function when it was obvious that the Oxford examiners would look to see something new given that the other submissions were older, the *Piano Quartet* from as far back as 1916, and *In Green Ways* (in the small orchestra version submitted) from 1928.

The *Fantasia* is Howells's biggest single span at some eighteen minutes playing time, and whilst every bar exclaims his authorship, the mood and general strength of purpose are not so familiar. There is considerable authority in this new language in which angst replaces more comfortable emotions. It has been pointed out before that he found 'pathos' in music one of its most powerful points of communication. He was a past master at writing music which took pathos to its limits. The *Elegy* is the most compelling early example. This *Fantasia*, however, is something different. First, it demonstrates his skills as an orchestrator. At no point is the cello – notoriously difficult to balance with a full orchestra – swamped by overblown gestures or muddy instrumental groupings, something for which Howells is often criticised. It is always allowed to sing freely, and it is not difficult to see why. This, of all the post-Michael (re)creations, is the single voice against the crowd, the singer articulating a still overwhelming grief. Here, if anywhere, one can see what Howells might have done if he had written a symphony, and what a crying shame it is that he did not. Put it with Christopher Palmer's outstanding orchestration of the completed slow movement of the *Concerto* (completed only in short score by Howells very soon after Michael's death) and imagine a third movement of corresponding dimensions, and one begins to get the feel of what Howells could have achieved in a work of almost Mahlerian proportions.

What many people find difficult with post-Michael Howells is the unrelenting nature of the grief in the music. It is important not to lose sight of the fact that the essence of both *Hymnus* and the *Fantasia* were written before Michael died, and there are interesting psychological inferences to be drawn from this concentration of sorrowful music written at a time when Howells was relatively care-free. It is almost as if, somewhere deep down, there was a prescience which subconsciously acknowledged that this music would have its purpose. There are other less fanciful reasons, too; first, simply a love of emotionally intense music; a reflection of world-wide mourning over horrific losses and waste in the Great War; and a feeling of inadequacy in himself in not being able to pull his weight, leaving his friends to fight on his behalf, some of whom were killed in the process. It is also perhaps notable, as we have discovered, and thinking of the more fanciful notion at the head of this list, that although the *Requiem* was written for Boris Ord and King's Cambridge Howells never sent it, and there was similarly no attempt to complete the *Concerto* or have it performed.

There is music to come, even of this period, which manages to free itself from the deepest of this obsession with grief, but almost everything is touched by the hem of the shroud which is ever-present. The real problem was Howells's lack of faith. As he told his daughter towards the end of his own life, he simply did not believe. Thus, he could not reconcile what had happened to Michael with a merciful God acting in his wisdom. Neither could he hope for any spiritual reunion with his son after his own death as he had no belief in an afterlife. Thus the sense of complete hopelessness which is such a feature of his elegiac music of this time (including the *Fantasia* and the *Concerto*'s slow movement), and thus also, the extraordinary nature of the one-off attempt at seeing purpose in loss: *Hymnus Paradisi*; where light pervades the whole score and we are led down a false trail, being made to believe that there really is a 'true light', which is 'passing wonderful'. In finding reasons for the positive nature of *Hymnus Paradisi* one must not underestimate the need which Howells felt to write 'comfort' music through the medium of appropriate words at this time. Indeed, it was precisely to try to assuage his grief through writing *about* Michael that Ursula suggested he compose this work. The inordinate amount of time Howells spent in church at this period, especially at Twigworth, says more about his emotional state, and his unwillingness to let go of the physical trappings of his son, than of any religious revelation or conversion. In fact, the 'holding on' to his son by having to be near him, underlines the flimsiness of his religious convictions.

The *Fantasia* is a big-boned, highly tensile, muscular work, a million miles away from the youthful fantasising of such orchestral pieces as the *Pastoral Rhapsody* or *Paradise Rondel*. The effect is of a sudden metamorphosis into maturity. While Howells may not have been able to see any point in his son's death, or have been able to reconcile himself to it through religious conviction, the outsider looking in, and from the vantage point of distance in time, might well be forgiven for feeling that there was indeed purpose in the boy's untimely end, but that to quote the poet Patrick Carey 'twas for thy sake'. It is as if a sacrifice was necessary in order to bring the best out of his father as a composer. This may all seem far-fetched. Quite possibly it is, and of course the boy had no choice in the matter. There is no doubt at all, however, that the music which Howells wrote after Michael's death found a wellspring of inspiration which had hitherto been missing in much of his work, and which brought a deep, often troubling, but nevertheless richly satisfying new edge to his music. No wonder the examiners at Oxford sought to make him one of their distinguished number when presented with this outstanding work – music which, although performed within his lifetime (it was first heard at St John's Smith Square, London in 1982), Howells was too old and infirm to properly appreciate. As for the *Threnody* as Christopher Palmer named it – the slow movement of the *Cello Concerto* – that was not heard until November 1992 in a centenary concert in Westminster Abbey.

Here, the unremitting grieving in the music, the slow, measured tread of the opening from which the cello begins its singing lamentation, is intensely moving. We know that Howells himself felt his early *Elegy* to be the ultimate expression of mourning. In that work he mourned the loss of a loved friend. Here, in the *Threnody*, the tragedy is magnified a hundred-fold, and this elegy is gut-wrenching in the intensity of its expression. It is, nevertheless, also mesmerisingly beautiful: the seemingly endless singing phrases, the richness of the harmonic language, the way the cello comes and goes in and out of the orchestral texture; all these things make what is effectively a love song in mourning. There is also something of the musical benediction here; the equivalent of the *Romanza* in Vaughan Williams's *Fifth Symphony*. There *is* in this *Threnody* (a 'song of lamentation' – Palmer names the piece aptly) an element of 'Romanza', but it is of a heart wrung out and bled dry of tears.

Whatever was now to happen in Howells's life, some feeling or representation of Michael would never be far beneath the surface. Another major score on which Howells had been working before Michael's death was the *Concerto for String Orchestra* written in response to the death of Sir Edward Elgar in 1934. It was given considerable added impetus by the tragic events in his own family, and the second movement became a joint commemoration of Elgar and Michael which Howells described as "submissive and memorial in its intention and purpose". Remembering how he had walked around the cloisters of Gloucester Cathedral with Elgar who had talked earnestly about writing for strings, Howells asked him "is there hope of ever acquiring the sheer sonority of string-writing, the sort that is yours?" Elgar replied "Yes. Study George Frederick (Handel) ... now and all your life" (CPC p. 403).

If Vaughan Williams's *Tallis Fantasia* was one beacon of light for Howells from way back in 1910, so Elgar's *Introduction and Allegro* for strings was another, heard for the first time only days later. These two works, so different and yet so complementary to each other, were seminal to Howells's development and to his own approach to writing for strings. The *Concerto* is his major contribution to the genre and shows just how much he had taken Elgar's advice to heart. It is a tour-de-force for strings, having two vibrant, virtuoso outer movements, the first of which was a complete reworking of the first movement of a *Suite for Strings* written in 1917. These were written to complement the already completed slow movement. Like the *Fantasia* for cello, this music is dark-hued; it may rise to elation, but it never achieves happiness, or is in any sense truly relaxed. Christopher Palmer in a note on the work for the Chandos recording (p.5) felt the work to be a "celebration-in-sound of West-of-England topography", but this is surely to read too much into it. Whilst Howells remained forever deeply attached to Gloucestershire, the music written at this critical time of his creative life becomes much less landscape-orientated, and as his titles demonstrate, are abstract in intention. No longer do we see such fanciful titles as *Paradise Rondel*; *Puck's Minuet*; *Pastoral Rhapsody*; *Jackanapes* and so on; we are now foursquare with concertos, suites, and titles which give away only the hints he allows as subtitles or dedications. It may still be said in Palmer's defence that title or no title, a Malvern outline is recognisable by suggestion whether by inference or explicit statement. Possibly. However, it is arguable that this music is raised well above mere topography by the abstract nature of its subject material and the sheer energy and drive of its motivation. Palmer relates this to "a great wind blowing off the mountains (the Malverns?)", but this is surely to belittle the larger vision of this work. It is also questionable as to whether or not it is helpful to put such pictures into the listener's mind – images which reduce the work to another pastoral idyll – even if there is fresh air blowing healthily through the score. It is also perhaps notable that Palmer cites the Malverns as his "mountains", albeit with a question mark. The very fact that the rolling hills of earlier works have now become mountains in the mind, indicates the metamorphosis which has taken place even over so short a period of time. Howells is climbing steeper inclines with far more rugged terrain than before, and it is therefore not surprising that his view from the top is more inclusive and far-sighted than the more domestic heights he was used to scaling before events overtook him.

The *Concerto* was completed in 1938 and dedicated to his lifelong friend Sir Adrian Boult, who conducted its first performance with the BBC orchestra in December that year. On 7 January 1939 Howells was back in the BBC studios for the first recording of the work with the same forces. After a few performances early in its life it then remained unperformed like much of Howells's orchestral music until Boult resurrected the work in 1974 and recorded it for EMI with the LPO.

Having finished his *Concerto*, Howells turned his mind once again to organ music and to a second set of *Psalm Preludes* (the first set was written between 1915 and 1916). It is plain to see just how far his style had travelled when the style of this second set of pieces is compared with that of the first. Almost inevitably, the casting-off point is another 'Michael' piece. Its text is from Psalm 130: 'Out of the deep have I called unto Thee, O Lord' (De profundis clamavi), and as the text implies, there are 'no holds barred' here. Howells lays his soul bare, and the searing emotion of the piece perhaps takes us closer to what he was really feeling than in any of the memorial pieces to date. Such raw emotion is rare and can, for instance, be seen in the opening cries of 'Michael'; in the *Sequence for St Michael* written as late as 1961. There really has been nothing like this in English organ music before. Yet, take the knowledge of the personal tragedy away, and it does not alter at all the power of the piece. It is simply one of the most passionate expositions in all organ music. The agonised declensions of twisted harmony which wind their way bitterly from extreme discord to unwilling concord as the piece treads its exhausted path to some sort of resolution, are as astonishing in their way, as the opening of the piece where the hands start at opposing ends of the keyboard and wind their sinewy way inwards. Only in the *Stabat Mater* (1963) did he again achieve, or perhaps try to achieve, such prolonged raw feeling in music.

The second Prelude is, by contrast, muted. It uses verse 11 of Psalm 139: 'If I say, surely the darkness shall cover me; even the night shall be light about me'. Even here, however, there is sombreness, and some sense of being spent after the passion of the first Prelude. The last of the set is a tour-de-force in which Howells tries (not very successfully) to banish the dark thoughts of the first two Preludes with a lighter and more positive finale based on verse 3 from Psalm 33: 'Sing unto Him a new song: play skilfully with a loud noise'. The opening chords – blue in character – set the tone for the whole work which has much jazz influence, but refined into a magnificent 'Sortie'. There are darker moments when the counterpoint winds like a snake in the grass, while the volume increases and the intensity rises. Intent on keeping his spirits up, however, back come the blue notes (sometimes outrageously on the tuba stop), bringing the work to an exciting and triumphant conclusion.

On 1 September 1939 Germany invaded Poland and on Sunday the third England and France declared war on Germany. The Howells family were staying at Lydney that week as, for the second time in his life, Howells was thrown into despair over the international situation. They stayed at Lydney until the twenty-fifth when they all returned to Barnes. The Russians had invaded Poland on Ursula's birthday, 17 September, and so the hostilities escalated with alarming speed. Outwardly, for the time being at least, Howells's life was not materially altered. He went on with his daily round of teaching at the RCM and St Paul's Girls' School. He continued his work as an examiner for the Associated Board, and he went on adjudicating at many local festivals all over the country. In the last quarter of 1939 alone he adjudicated in Bingley, Leicester, Derby, Blackpool, Keighley, Kingston, Southend and Taunton. He was a popular and highly successful adjudicator and it was no surprise that he was so much in demand.

Howells's great strengths as an adjudicator were his overall fairness and sense of encouragement, and his command of the English language. David Willcocks, who often adjudicated with him, remembered: "He would have something good to write about each of them, never repeating himself, and he would go up at the end and sum up a class with great clarity giving them something positive to work for so they could improve on their performances another time. The sort of thing I do remember after all these years was the little girl who got up and sang a very simple little song and I wrote down on my mark sheet 'pretty voice' and I looked over my shoulder to see what he had written and he had put 'a voice of dewy freshness', and I wish that I had thought of a phrase like that because it did just describe that girl's voice" (BBC/Green). Sir Keith Falkner, Director at the RCM in the mid 1960s and early 1970s, underlined this by saying: "There was no hyperbole, there was no saying 'at the end of the day'; 'what's left on the table' – nothing was ever wasted, every word meant something" (ibid).

Howells explained his own reasons for spending so much of his life at this particular coalface in this way: "That was largely an offshoot of my infancy and the sort of people I met. I wanted to get amongst the ordinary people, the ordinary lovers of music rather than the extraordinarily gifted ones. You can't do without your Vaughan Williamses and Elgars and people obviously, but you can make the fundamental mistake of living without being in touch with the people that really matter" (ibid).

Creatively, Howells's mind was working on two strands at this time, moving backwards and forwards between organ music and music for string orchestra. It was an extremely fruitful time, and barring some very fine early chamber music from his student days, was further proof of accession to a remarkable period of maturity in his composition. It is not possible to account for this fundamental change without the knowledge that he was feeding off recent tragic events. It further underlines the argument of purpose in tragedy. Howells will have been too close to it to see this, but had he been able to think objectively about his own creative resurgence and the reasons for it, he might at least have felt that some good had come out of it, which may, in its own small way, have been a crumb of comfort.

The year 1939 saw the start of a new series of pieces for organ collectively called *Six Pieces for Organ*. The first to be written was the *Fugue, Chorale and Epilogue*. By now Howells's style of organ writing displayed all the originality and personality which his younger contemporary in France, Maurice Duruflé, was showing in his own way. Both were entirely original, and both writing within the 'schools' they represented. In this work, a long-breathed fugue builds up to a passionate statement of the chorale which is gradually let down over a lengthy pedal point into a nagging Epilogue which eventually sees resolution.

Almost as soon as this piece was completed Howells began work on *Master Tallis's Testament* which became No.3 of the set. This piece is actually far more important in Howells's list of works than its meagre five minutes playing time would indicate. He regarded it as one of his favourite compositions, and as a 'footnote' to Vaughan Williams's *Tallis Fantasia*. In fact Howells was entering another period when Tudor/Elizabethan dances and dance forms were providing the inspiration for many of his works. A new set of clavichord pieces was imminent, and several of these *Six Pieces for Organ* were related in one way or another to music of the earlier period. There were two Sarabands, a *Sine Nomine* (a work like his 1922 choral and orchestral piece of the same name, implying relationship with the old 'In Nomine' form, and being a piece of simply outstanding impressionistic colouring), and, of course, *Master Tallis*.

New Year's Day 1941 saw the Howells family once again at Gloucester and at "Twigworth, to Mick 3.20" followed by tea with Canon Cheesman. They went on to visit the Sumsions in Gloucester before spending the night, and the next week, at Lydney. On Sunday the seventh, Howells spent the afternoon with Lord Bledisloe at Lydney Park. What a turn-around in his fortunes since the days when as a boy he was sent to the kitchen on arrival! On Thursday the eleventh Howells visited Herbert Sumsion and they played through the proofs which had just arrived of the second set of *Psalm Preludes*. He also showed Sumsion the recently completed *Fugue, Chorale and Epilogue* and *Master Tallis's Testament*, two of the *Six Pieces* which he was to dedicate as a set to Sumsion.

He returned to London to a life of febrile activity which included a performance of his *Concerto for Strings* at the Aeolian Hall on 30 January. On 5 February he took Ursula to see Vaughan Williams at a performance of *Gerontius* at the Albert Hall, where he sat next to the Archbishop of Canterbury. Even at this stage of his celebrity,

Howells cannot resist noting important people with whom he came into contact.

In the meantime the war was raging on, and on 9 April 1940 Hitler invaded Norway and Sweden. On the tenth Howells noted: "Anxiety everywhere". More importantly still, however, comes Friday the twelfth: "Beloved Mick's birthday anniversary. (He wd have been 14.) D and I went to Twigworth... April colours!". Then the very next day Howells fell ill. The doctor (Dowling) was called, and on the fifteenth, pleurisy was diagnosed. This was an illness which, although the Graves disease with which he had been afflicted in his youth was long past, was taken very seriously. On the twenty-first a specialist, Maurice Davidson, was called and he ordered x-rays. Feeling he might be improving a little, Howells was out of bed briefly the next day, but went straight back again, and was taken to Brompton Hospital for further x-rays on the twenty-fifth. As May dawned, so things continued their uneven path. On the seventh, his temperature began rising, peaking at 100.2 on the twelfth, Whit Sunday. On the tenth, Germany had invaded Holland, Belgium and Luxemburg, and Howells noted again "a grave feeling everywhere". It was not until 26 May that his temperature finally returned to normal and he ventured out of the house for the first time since illness had seized him some six weeks earlier. One of his first actions was to go to Kensington for a haircut. Appearance was everything.

So much was now disrupted because of the ongoing and developing hostilities, and on this front things were moving apace. Italy declared war on 10 June; France asked for armistice on the seventeenth and signed a week later; the Bournemouth Festival at which Howells was to have adjudicated was cancelled, and for the first time he was present in an air raid when in Weymouth on 11 July. At 3am the next day he was woken by another, and for the last time in his diaries we see him attending a concert in the Queen's Hall given by the LPO on 18 July. Air raids soon caught up with him in London, and the fifteenth saw the Germans attacking Croydon when the Howells family heard the sirens sound at 7.10 p.m. whilst taking a walk at the Round Pond in Barnes.

Little did they think how closely the war would come to affect them later that same year. Howells wrote to the conductor and composer Julius Harrison in December 1941:

> Our house was blitzed and bashed and ruined one awful night in Sept of 1940. Ursula was mercifully in Scotland (and has been there ever since as a busy and acting member of the highly-competent Dundee Repertory Company). D and I were visiting a brother-in-law that night in Sanderstead – and only by that lucky chance escaped pretty certain death. Our part of Barnes was simply devastated – for no military cause whatsoever.
>
> Homeless we sought refuge in Cheltenham for sometime, I going to and fro' London where Dyson gave me a 'bedroom' in the basement of the RCM – with himself and Sammons and Topliss Green for occasional companions.
>
> Now D and I have taken a small furnished house (No.11, Beverley Close) – again on Barnes Common. Perhaps that'll bring on a new London Blitz! It has been a divided and desultory year... but many of one's friends have been worse hit – no use grumbling therefore!
> (LF p.247)

In fact there was plenty of reason to grumble, and some reason for all of us to regret the bombing of that house. All Howells's library was lost that day, together with manuscripts, books and scores. No one knows how much original material was destroyed. It is a tragic waste, reminiscent of Howells's dinner with A.E. Housman all those years before, after which he destroyed so many songs.

New Year 1941 saw the Howells family snowed up in Cheltenham, but as ever Howells put the time to the best possible use. Every day until 15 January when he returned to London, something new was achieved. On new year's day he scored a movement from a *Folk Tune Set* he had recently completed in short score. This movement was the second (of three) and set the tune of *St Louis of France*, a fifteenth-century melody of which Howells was extremely fond, and which he had been given many years before by Edwin Evans. Howells later showed it to Ravel in the hope that he would use it "in his own unique way", saying "here, surely, is your ancestry", but Ravel never did (CPC pp.439-40).

On 2 January Howells copied the newly completed score and

noted that the snow continued to fall. The next day saw him beginning a two-piano arrangement of the *Triumph Tune* for solo piano which he had written in 1934 and was intended then to be orchestrated as the first movement of this *Folk Song Set*. It continued to snow as he also set the questions that day for the B.Mus examinations the following March for Durham University. The day after that (4 January) he posted the full scores of the *St Louis Tune* and *Old Mole* (the *Folk Song Set's* third movement) to the BBC.

On the 5 January he began a series of anthems which he described as being *In Time of War*, and here he probably referred back in his mind to Haydn's *Mass In Tempore Bellae*. Two of these anthems were to be amongst his most popular and enduring works for the church. Each one of the series was written within a single day, and the set began with *O Pray for the Peace of Jerusalem*. This was followed on 6 January by *Ponder my Words* (the MS of which is now missing except for the title page). The third anthem, *We have heard with our ears* was written whilst more snow fell on 7 January; while the next day, Wednesday, saw feverish activity with *Like as the Hart* being written at a single sitting, followed by sketches for the first movement of a new *Suite for Strings* for St Paul's Girls' School. The day after that Howells set his fifth anthem *Great is the Lord*, but interrupted by air raids, he did not complete it until 2am. Undaunted by a short night, he completed the first movement of the *St Paul's Suite* later the same day (10 January), making notes for the second movement on Saturday and finishing it on the Sunday. Without pause for breath, the next movement of *the Suite* was under way on 13 January and completed the day after before he returned to London at 9 a.m. on the day after that. All this was remarkable activity by any standards, and it is a great shame that it would seem that only the sketches of the strings work have survived.

On 11 March 1941 Walford Davies died "after three days of illness (near Bristol) – God rest him!". Howells had learnt much about choral technique from Walford Davies when he was a student at the RCM, and it was his old teacher's *Requiem* for unaccompanied voices which had provided the model for Howells's own back in 1934.

Once again not able to materially assist in the war effort, though less guiltily this time because of his age, Howells nevertheless took his turn in doing fire-watching duty, helping to spread the alarm the moment a fire was detected as a result of enemy action. On Good Friday, 11 April 1941, he took his turn of duty between 2 and 5 a.m. on the roof of the RCM and spent much of the time reading plainsong! The next day ("Beloved Michael would have been 15 today") he was copying the In *Time of War* anthems to which he added another the following day, *Let God Arise*, a setting of Psalm 68. More fire-watching duties continued through the night and he noted baldly on the following Wednesday that "London's worst air-raid began at 9 p.m.". The day after that he noted that "the raid continued till 4.30 a.m." and that there was the "sound of sweeping glass everywhere".

And so 1941 wound its wearisome way forward. Life continued in its disfigured way whilst war raged on, Howells still noting major events in his diary as they occurred: 10 May: "Great raid on London. Hess landed by parachute near Glasgow". 22 June: "The astonishing news that Hitler had invaded Russia" and so on. Proof positive that all five anthems were indeed completed (including at that stage *Great is the Lord* but less the sixth *Let God Arise* just written and in due course to be substituted) comes in a diary entry for Friday 27 June when Howells noted that he "shewed Tom Armstrong the 5 Anthems *In Time of War*."

Also at this time, Howells was starting work on another set of Clavichord pieces, this time to be called *Howells' Clavichord*, originally published in two volumes but later (in 1978) amalgamated into one. The first pieces he wrote were *Benjamin's Brawl* and *Bax's Jewell* – neither of which were eventually included. Next came *Walton's Toye* on 15 August, the exuberant piece which was to close Volume 2. *Patrick's Pavane* on the twenty-fifth (to become *Patrick's Siciliano*) was followed the next day by *Jacob's Fancy* (to become *Jacob's Brawl*). On 8 September Howells went up to Wood Norton to hear the broadcast of the first five of his *Howells' Clavichord*: 'Benjy', Walford, Boult, Paddy (Hadley), and Walton. Of these, 'Benjy' and 'Walford' did not make it to final publication.

A renewal of an old friendship had preceded this event when, on 27 August, Howells and his wife were in Lydney "organ-ising at

Lydney church with L[eslie] and N[eil – his son] – and Great Baxter". Baxter was, of course, the tin plate worker/organist from all those years before when Howells was a boy.

Three days later Howells was invited to lunch at St John's College, Cambridge and was asked to consider assuming the role of acting organist of the college whilst Robin Orr, the regular organist, was away on active service in the RAF. He returned there on 17 September, Ursula's nineteenth birthday, to have tea with the Dean, Mr Raven, and the President of the college, Mr Charlesworth. On the twenty-fifth he formally accepted the post. Yet another major strand to add to his hectic life and work load, but one which also proved to be another major turning point in his creative life, and one which, in some ways, was to prove the most important of all.

EIGHT
Cambridge and Canticles

Howells's term at Cambridge effectively started on Friday 3 October 1941 when he spent most of the day there practising the organ at St John's. And practice he must have needed as he told Julius Harrison in a letter dated 9 December:

> ... you're not the only musical Methuselah crawling up organ-loft steps these days, or persuading leg-muscles to recall their pedalling acts of 20 or 30 years ago, or making the seat of his trousers 50% more shiny than they were before the war inter-fered with the decencies of our careers. The fact is, I myself have been doing all these things since early October – at St John's College, Cambridge: Rootham's old place. Latterly their man has been Robin Orr (who was at Leeds for a time) – and he's in the RAF now. I'm still rubbing my eyes about it: seems absurd for me to be 'in church' again after being out of organ lofts for 24 years. (Salisbury was the last – 1917!)
>
> I've been given the status and privileges of a Fellow of St John's: and a suite of rooms: and free dinners in Hall etc, etc. in addition to my pay. I go down to Cambridge on Thursday evening and return to London on early Monday morning, each week.
>
> (LF p.247)

And so Howells fell on his feet with the ideal war-time job and, as we have seen before, was not above 'crowing' to his friends about his good fortune. Wonderful surroundings, intelligent company, contact with church music again, and yet little real responsibility as he was only 'acting' organist. Thursday 9 October was the day when things really got going. He was allocated rooms: H1 on the first floor of H staircase in Second Court, a suite of rooms which included its own bathroom, a rarity in those days, but something he had insisted on. The President of the College called to see him inviting him to breakfast the next morning. At 9.15 a.m. he took his first boys' practice. This started a busy day, which took him to the University Press; to lunch with his nephew Neil (who, as a student at Queen Mary's College, London reading Physics, had been evacuated to King's College Cambridge at this time); to the chapel for further organ practice; and to King's chapel where Harold Darke, who was acting organist there, was preparing for a broadcast. They had tea together and Howells then returned to St John's for dinner in Hall.

The next day he had breakfast in his rooms, took the boys for a lengthy practice lasting from 9.15 to 10.55 a.m., returned to his rooms for lunch, and took a full choir practice at 5.30 p.m. On his first Sunday he noted "a happy first day's services". And so the pattern was set for the next four years.

Sir John Margetson and John Williams, two of Howells's choral scholars ('choral students' as they are called at St John's) remember well Howells's approach to his life in Cambridge. John Margetson tells that he always liked to dine in Hall "and thereafter would sometimes entertain three or four of us undergraduates to coffee in his rooms... A particular reason for dining in Hall, so he told me, was to extract from the don sitting next to him an account of the latest work being done in any particular academic field. This would then form the basis of his Monday lecture at the Royal College of Music, which, in accordance with Parry's wish to broaden the minds of music students, was on any subject other than music" (JM/CR). Howells was very lucky with the Fellows with whom he was able to have these lengthy discussions at St John's. Amongst the closest of them was Max Newman, a distinguished mathematician who was currently working at Bletchley on ciphering. He was also an amateur musician with an extraordinary natural ability who played the whole of Bach's '48' in concerts at the College. Howells's other great friend was Martin Charlesworth, the President of the College, who was a classics scholar and another excellent pianist with whom Howells frequently played duets.

As a boy at Blundell's John Margetson was encouraged by his Director of Music to become an organ scholar at Cambridge. As luck would have it, his chosen course ruled this out. However, it was possible for him to be a choral scholar, and after last-minute vocal training he went up for the examination, which took place in Boris Ord's rooms in King's. After lunch he was told to go into King's chapel to sing his solo pieces. Inspired by his surroundings he gave of his best, and was awarded a scholarship to St John's. It is important to realise that St John's choir in those days was not the well-oiled professional machine it is today. It was a weekend choir only, and had lay clerks as well as students singing in the back rows. Being 'professionals', the lay clerks took any solo work which was needed, and this meant that the choral scholars did not get a great deal of experience. Indeed sometimes the young choral scholars felt rather superfluous, and Margetson described how the bass lay-clerk next to whom he had to stand used to "boom out like a tuba stop!". The choir had a small repertoire and they did absolutely nothing by Howells in all the four years of his tenure.

Howells was apparently very kind to the choral scholars. They were all much in awe of him as by now he was absolutely at the height of his powers, and his reputation was thoroughly established. His appointment was certainly a coup for St John's. John Margetson remembers clearly how well ordered Howells was. He would wear a 'uniform', always turning up in a dark suit, a blue shirt and a red tie, and he would speak in a precise, well-modulated way. This seemed also to apply to his bearing, and to the way he walked. Herbert Sumsion also remarked on Howells's appearance: "He always seemed to be doing things quickly, he moved quickly around College, and if he were catching a bus he would more than likely run for it although it wasn't perhaps necessary. I think to a certain extent he was a bit highly strung, a bit strung up if you like. As a teacher I should have thought very good if the person concerned was any good. I don't know whether he had the patience to deal with people who possibly hadn't got much ability. In that case I think he would probably talk to them about cricket or even about his own works" (BBC/Prizeman).

Returning to his life in Cambridge, he would very often spend his evenings with his old friends Boris Ord, Philip Radcliffe and Patrick Hadley. Ord was recently back in Cambridge and had resumed the reins of the University Musical Society, (though not King's), taking back control from Hadley who had looked after it while he was away. It was also pleasant for Howells to have his old friend Darke at King's for this period, even though Darke's tenure (a war-time arrangement like his own) was not, by all accounts, as smooth-running as his own, and indeed came rather unkindly to be called "the dark ages". Margetson also remembers the ubiquitous pretty girls who peppered Howells's life at this time. He and some other Cambridge students used to go to London to see him at College, as he (rather bluntly) put it "partly to see him, and partly in the knowledge that the prettiest girls in the College would be either there (in Howells's room) or thereabouts. He was well known to love pretty girls, and we were quite happy to use him as a sort of high-class pimp!" (JM/PS).

There are a number of things which remain indelibly imprinted on Margetson's mind from this time: one was Howells saying "the chord of the open 5th is like an open bottle, you never know what can be poured into it". He also remembers that Howells would always leave a score of Warlock's 'The Curlew' on the piano in his room at the RCM at this time, after someone who had been using his room had made disparaging remarks about Warlock's music to him. This is an interesting observation on Howells's attitude to fellow composers, for he regarded Warlock the man with complete contempt. However, as a composer and scholar, he held him in the highest regard, and would not allow personal issues to cloud his judgement of Warlock as a creative artist.

John Williams well remembers Howells improvising before services in St John's, although he also asserts that Howells did sometimes play pieces after the services. He remembers Howells taking Bach's *Orgelbüchlein* into chapel to practise, which he normally did early on Sunday mornings. When he did improvise, which was often, Williams felt that he always used these occasions to try things out, and that extended cadences were always a notable feature of whatever Howells was playing. Felix Aprahamian also remembered the fabled playing: "I was surprised, or perhaps I wasn't too surprised, to learn that during the whole of his period there he never played a piece of printed organ music, and this is a clue to his own organ music. It has the quality of an improvisation, it's very difficult to grasp, it's pretty difficult to analyse, it's rather free and it is rhapsodic" (BBC/Prizeman). John Williams remembered Howells's keyboard technique as "funny, but he got around the notes. It was rather like the technique you use for playing Couperin, without thumbs, in a way – lumpy". He also described his conducting technique as "meticulous, precise and too fussy. He tried to beat every note" (JW/PS).

Choral music on the chapel lists was straightforward, and the staple fare included canticles such as *Walmisley in d minor*, *Rootham in e minor* (Rootham "the good Doctor" had been organist of St John's before Robin Orr), *Alan Gray in G*, *Wood in e flat*, *Martin Shaw in c minor* and *Boyce in A*. Anthems included *Tristis* by Lassus, *Adoramus Te* by Palestrina, Purcell's *Remember not, O Lord, our Offences*, and *Sing Joyfully* by Mundy.

Perhaps it was this vivid reminder of how second-rate church music could be, particularly in relation to the canticles listed above, which planted the seeds in his mind that led to his completely rewriting the rules for Anglican church music. This can be put beside the letter he wrote to Harold Darke (see pages 50-51 above) following news of his appointment to Salisbury. "I have talked to you often enough of the sort of repugnance which even some of the best church music kindled in me – merely because it all filtered through that nasty mood which has been part of my musical mentality since Gloucester". As if this was not enough, he went on to say that he wanted to "build up a healthier and happier set of associations than those which my life at Gloucester produced, and which have played such havoc with that part of my musical state of mind which had relation to church music."

Two things flow from this in relation to his work at St John's. First, he was positively able to engender a 'healthier and happier set of associations' for all those who passed through his hands in the choir at the College. Both Williams and Margetson testify to the encouragement Howells gave to the whole choir, and in particular to the boys and the students. This latter group, as we have seen, were often invited to Howells's rooms, and frequently stayed late into the night discussing all sorts of subjects over coffee and drinks. It was a stimulating time for both parties. Second, the close encounter with church music not only at the time of his creative maturity, but also in this early post-Michael period, undoubtedly led him to consider ways of contributing in a more positive way to enriching the church repertoire. The real watershed of *Collegium Regale* is still some three years away, but the people and the place were working hard on him, though subconsciously as yet.

Cambridge became the dominant force in Howells's life for some time. He did not, however, ignore the imperatives of the RCM and St Paul's Girls' School. Nor did he apparently reduce his work for the Associated Board or local festivals, but much was disrupted by the war, and all these things were operating on a reduced capacity at this time.

As 1941 drew to a close, so all the usual end-of-term Christmas events caught everyone up with their feverish festive feeling. On 28 November Howells played a group of his new clavichord pieces in a small-scale concert in the Combination Room at St John's, and on 8 December he organised a concert in chapel given by the choir accompanied by string orchestra, with Harold Darke playing the organ. Included in the programme was Vaughan Williams's *Fantasia on Christmas Carols*. There was little hope of keeping cheerful for long however, as the news from the hostilities was becoming increasingly depressing. Roosevelt was asking the US Congress for a declaration of war on Japan who, the previous day, had attacked the Americans and British in the Far East. England declared war on Japan the following day, and on 10 December, there was deepening gloom as the news came in of the sinking of the 'Prince of Wales' and the 'Repulse' in Singapore. On the eleventh Germany and Italy declared war on the USA, and Howells noted in his diary "USA reciprocated. A world gone mad!"

However, apart from his fire-watching duties, Howells kept up a relatively normal existence and the war did not materially affect him any more than anyone else of his age. The Goossens family, one of those remarkable dynasties in music, had all been contemporaries of his as students at the RCM. Eugene was fêted as one of the leading conductor/composers of the day; his sisters Sidonie and Marie, two of the great harpists; and Leon one of the world's finest oboe players. It was inevitable that Leon Goossens would inspire composers to write music for him, and that is how Howells came to write his *Sonata for oboe and piano* in 1942.

After a run of extraordinary works, white-hot in their passionate intensity, and all partly fulfilling their cathartic purpose, it must have come as something of a shock to find on delivery (August 1942) that Goossens 'had serious reservations about the structure of the work'. Howells said that he would 'have another go at it', but he never did, and the music was so completely buried and unknown that it did not appear in any lists of works, and only came to light when Christopher Palmer unearthed it when writing his study of Howells three decades later (CPS).

The *Sonata* is a major four-movement work, and performances and recordings by both Nicholas Daniel with Julius Drake, and Sarah Francis with Peter Dickinson have proved what an important addition this work is to the oboe repertory. As usual Howells's reticence, and his unwillingness to trust his own judgement when faced with adverse critical appraisal of his music, led to a complete loss of interest in the work.

As was so often the case, there is some recycling of earlier material in the *Sonata*. The 'Lento' slow movement is a much revised version of one of his early songs *O Garlands Hanging by the Door* dating from 1920. He so successfully binds the music into the scheme of things that it is impossible to tell that it is from his first period of composition, the year of his marriage and *Merry Eye*. He uses the end of the movement to great effect in bringing it back again at the end of the whole *Sonata*. One wonders whether Goossens was really *so* unhappy about the structure of the work that he did not want to play it. Although this may be heresy to oboe players who have revered him over many years, he may simply have found it unplayable. One of Howells's traits which singers find such a problem is the inordinate length of his phrases. He seems to want a seamless flow of melody, and is perhaps harking back to the endless flow of plainsong, or the flow created by the interplay of voices through counterpoint. This presents considerable obstacles for wind players and singers alike. This *Sonata* has many examples of this, and Goossens may well have been faced with something the like of which he had not met before in the oboe repertory. To witness a performance now is not only to realise the challenges with which Howells faces his players. It is also to understand his vision in seeing beyond current technical achievements to a time when players (and singers) would cope with the heavy, but rewarding, demands placed on them. Certainly the fact that this *Sonata* waited for its first performance until 1984 (unrevised, though not without hints in the manuscript of possible changes), shows just how far playing had developed in the intervening forty years. The shelving of this work may, in fact, have served another purpose. There are so many similarities, and yet fundamental differences, between the *Oboe Sonata* and the one he wrote for Clarinet only four years later, that Howells may have seen the *Clarinet Sonata* as itself the revision of the earlier work, and was content to leave the *Oboe Sonata* buried.

On 10 September 1942 George Dyson, Director of the RCM, wrote to Howells: "My dear Herbert, You'll get a printed chit next week announcing certain changes of rooms here, but as yours is one of the most essential, I want to give you reasons for the scheme. We are going to shut up most of the top floor. It is the only way of easing a very acute and growing domestic shortage. We shall use your present room, but only for 'casuals' and occasionally. We have given you 19, which you will have undisturbed for all your days, with Jacob next door and Morris across the corridor. There is a piano problem too, but this is indirect in effect. I am going to shut up the best piano rooms, except strictly for lessons, and try to preserve the few good ones we have. We shall get no more while the war lasts. You'll find 19 sunny and as quiet as there is, if less near heaven! Yours ever, GD". And so Room 19 in the first floor basement became Howells's for the rest of his career (Dyson and his successors were as good as his word on that score), and the point of welcome for generations of music students.

In 1942 Howells seemed to wake up to his advancing years, and for only the second time in his diaries he records his age on his birthday.

In 1941 he had noted that he was 49, and then in 1942 that RVW reached his seventieth and Howells his fiftieth in the same week (Vaughan Williams's birthday was on 12 October). Exactly a month before his, Ursula had reached her own milestone in celebrating her twentieth birthday.

The year 1943 was a fallow one, composition-wise. Life was taken up with the regular fixtures in his life, and a great deal of broadcasting work for the BBC, including programmes for schools. His old friend Arthur Bliss was now head of music at the BBC, and called upon Howells's services frequently to enrich the music programme in his inimitable way. Howells's beautiful speaking voice was ideal for radio broadcasting, his command of the language was second to none, and his enormous experience of teaching and lecturing gave him real insight into what people found interesting. Howells was often a guest at special BBC functions, too, and on one memorable occasion was asked to a concert given by the BBC orchestra in the Maida Vale studios. Menuhin was to be the soloist in the Bartok Concerto and was so exhausted by his constant travelling to play to the troops in morale-boosting tours, that during this concert, whenever there was a long enough pause in the solo part, he would stand on his head and practise his Yoga exercises. A doubtless alarming experience for all present.

It is somehow fitting that possibly the most sublime piece of architecture in England, the chapel at King's College Cambridge, should be the launching pad for the twentieth century's equivalent in music for the church. Howells, Hadley, Ord and Dean Milner-White (so soon to be appointed Dean of York) were having tea in Ord's rooms in King's when things took an extraordinary turn. Discussion focused on settings of the *Te Deum* and Howells continues the story:

> My concern was more directly related to King's College, its Dean, Organist, and superb singing in the lovely chapel; and of one unique origin – a simple bet, made at a tea-for-four in Dr Boris Ord's. The Dean of King's fixed the terms of the bet, he who was soon to be the Very Reverend the Dean of York. There were two 'young' composers present; the bet was aimed at them. The Organist was the Witness, Host and Holder of the Stakes. One of the composers ultimately failed to win the Dean's betric

guinea – but he did become, later, Professor of Music in the University of Cambridge. The other did a *Te Deum* to satisfy conditions; it was later to become known as *Collegium Regale* – the only *Te Deum* to be born of a decanal bet. And Cambridge heard King's College Choir give the first performance in 1944.
(CPC p.401)

One guinea! If ever there was a musical bargain, this must be it. For that one guinea kickstarted music for the Anglican church into a whole new phase of existence. Milner-White was remarkably prescient to single out Howells as the man for the job. That he was 'waiting in the wings', and had so obviously found his vocation, was noted with pride in a letter to Howells that Milner-White wrote when he arrived at York: "By these last two services of yours (*Collegium Regale* and the *Gloucester Service*), I personally feel that you have opened a wholly new chapter in Service, perhaps in Church, music. Of *spiritual* moment rather than liturgical. It is so much more than music-making; it is experiencing deep things in the only medium that can do it. I cannot help hoping that you will give yourself with renewed hope & vision to compsition in a field in which – may I say it? – you can create *masterworks*" (CPC p.168).

At the time Howells began seriously to write church music, the biggest step forward of the earlier generation had been taken by his own teacher, Charles Villiers Stanford. In their day, Stanford's settings were as mould-breaking as Howells's, and still represent a high water mark of twentieth-century music for the Anglican church. Stanford approached his canticles almost symphonically, and indeed a number of them were conceived with orchestral accompaniment. Each new set of canticles was given a completely new character. Whether painting the picture of Mary at her spinning wheel in the G major set, or touching grandeur in the C major set, or, again, coming close to a choral rhapsody in the A major canticles, the originality and quality of Stanford's music has ensured their enduring popularity to this day.

Howells's canticle settings would have been 'modern stinks' to Stanford who would not have understood their point of departure. In starting with the *Te Deum* and *Jubilate* for King's, Howells did not nail all his colours to the mast at once. In fact, for the arch-impressionist amongst English composers, the big-scale *Te Deum* is remarkably *de point*. Particularly unusual in much of this work is the fact that so little of it is overtly contrapuntal. The first page and a half is in unison, and the first three pages almost entirely homophonic, at least as far as the voices are concerned. Part of the skill of this setting is in the fact that the organ supplies much of the counterpoint with the voices and so acts both as a 'gelling agent' of continuity and flow in the music. Once the initial statements have been made, so Howells allows melismas (the setting of a number of notes to one syllable) to colour important words. It is instructive to see which words Howells regards as important in this context: 'praise'; 'infinite'; 'glory' (several times, and easily given the most extensive melismas) and 'everlasting'. This then gives a clue to the way in which Howells's mind is responding and reacting to stimuli in the text. He comes at the music vertically rather than horizontally: Christ in his glory and mystery, rather than Jesus, friend and brother. There are no surprises here: first; Howells's impressionistic style suits perfectly the 'mystery' in religious texts: second; not being a believer himself, he responds simply to the beauty of words and the powerful imagery; third, his harmonic language and the brilliance of his contrapuntal skills set him up perfectly to woo the listener into being ravished one minute, and gently chastised the next. It is an extraordinary balancing act carried out with almost unerring good taste, and yet with a real desire to enrich people's lives by adding a degree of contemporary beauty in the music they are hearing which has been hitherto almost unknown. It is exactly the same principle as the building of Oxford Movement (high church) churches in the very poorest areas of towns and cities in the Victorian period. The introduction into ordinary people's deprived lives of something of order, colour and remark to which they could not only relate, but feel was also feeding them spiritually, and which also attempted to make sense of their pitiful existences, had to be an influence for good.

Impressionist colouring is certainly in evidence in this first *Te Deum*, and not just in the matter of ecstatic melismas. The phrase which states "We believe that thou shalt come to be our judge" is given (non-imitative) contrapuntal treatment, the staggered entries of which imply nervous acquiescence of the fact. Add to this a long pedal point in the organ part, indicated to be played with the 32' stop drawn, and the listener is left literally shaking. The end of the work, where the injunction is for us never to "be confounded", has a wonderful sense of power and confidence. Howells knew very well both the power of music to influence and persuade, and it begins where the spoken word leaves off. To this extent, believer or not, his was to become a ministry in music as profound as anything to be written by the greatest theologians or tub-thumping evangelical preachers.

The *Jubilate* which goes with the E flat *Te Deum* setting is, quite remarkably, in E flat *minor*. Here is a text which reads: "O be joyful in the Lord all ye lands: serve the Lord with gladness, and come before His presence with a song". But here, once again, we have a clear pointer to Howells's approach to text setting. Words such as 'joyful' or 'gladness' do not imply levity or gaity. It is all part of this 'vertical' versus 'horizontal' approach. Thus, we should feel privileged as Christ's disciples to praise Him; and so, for *privileged* read *joyful* and so on. It is perfectly appropriate, therefore, that joy should be registered in a minor key – and what a minor key! This wrap-your-arms-around-it key must be the richest and darkest of all, and there is something immensely comforting in it, almost especially because it is in the minor. Whilst once again noting a quite straightforward approach to the choral writing, there are also the melismas which occur, and the gentle playing with rhythm where 3/4 can be dancingly interchangeable with 6/8 – Howells perhaps raising just an eyebrow in acknowledgement of the Psalm's character. With the *Gloria*, however, he puts us firmly back where we started with the dark hues of E flat minor, and an extraordinarily long and low final E flat for the choir whilst the organ pounds its way to the end including, in one edition, an all-engulfing passage for the tuba stop.

What one sees most is Howells's sensitivity to language, and his thoughtful approach to the syllabic stresses in the text. Everything is worked out so that the words can be sung almost as if they were spoken, without losing any of their natural flow. Melismas are natural embellishments which allow us moments of ecstatic repose in the flow of the text, and give Howells the opportunity to voice the listener's own desire to be 'transported' at key moments.

The extraordinary thing about this new phase in Howells's life was his very real sense of vocation and that he should have taken so long to come to it. Yes, he had written church music before, but the sheer volume of work he undertook in this medium from this point until virtually the end of his life, marked him out as the greatest contributor to the music of the Anglican church this century. Appropriately, he served as President of the Friends of Cathedral Music for twenty-four years.

Gloucester, in his childhood and youth, had been a two-edged sword. That important letter to Darke shows Howells's time there was not happy, leaving him with mixed feelings about church music in cathedrals. Salisbury was too brief an interlude, and too coloured by his illness, to set the record straight. No wonder, then, that he concentrated his efforts in that early period on chamber and orchestral music, songs and music for solo instruments. It took the sea-change of his son's death followed by his extremely happy period at St John's, Cambridge, when he seemed almost as much involved at King's, to unlock the best of what had always been in him from Gloucester days and allow the real inspiration to flow.

His own 'credo' can be read into a list of concerns he voiced when writing in *English Church Music* in 1966: "It may be that the future of English Church-and-Cathedral music is hedged with difficulties and doubts. I fear the gross threat of a 'pepping-up', the cheap surrender to popularity, the insidious and melodramatic 'putting down the mighty from their seat', tonal elephantiasis encouraged by the misuse of outsize organs, the careless denial of idiomatic fitness. These are inherent dangers. They must be countered by men of genius who from time to time shall offer the Church works of supreme fitness" (ECM 1966).

'Fitness' was a word Howells used often and underlined his fundamental feeling for taste and dignity. His style in his music for the church has often been described as successful because it marries spirituality with sensuality. It is a tightrope to walk, especially given Howells's own stated reservations listed above. Yet, if the word 'sensuality' is not misconstrued, it can easily be seen that what is really intended is spiritual ecstasy, the building-up of emotional tension in the music which acts like an electrical charge and, when well performed, imprints itself on the mind of the listener with searing intensity. The effect on the first to hear this music, which is now so familiar to us yet still no less impressive, must have had some of the power of the great medieval churches rising above the hovels of the local population. Howells once said of Stanford's great motet *Beati Quorum Via*: "Let that motet stand for works that by any criteria are not only highly accomplished, but profoundly human and of sur-passing fitness" (CPC p.291). That word 'fitness' again; but also the acknowledgement that what produced it was also 'profoundly human'. Howells, as we have seen time and again, was profoundly human. Whichever way you look at it, he was a sensualist, but this was tempered in his work by a huge intellect, a wide-ranging deep knowledge of literature, and also an innate good taste.

It must not be thought that when Howells began his *Collegium Regale* settings, the musical language he used was new-born. One only has to look at that tiny masterpiece from as recently as 1941 *Like as the hart desireth the waterbrooks* to see that something was brewing in his mind. This piece also refutes once and for all the often-stated allegation that Howells could not write a tune. The opening section for the tenors and basses must be amongst the most wonderfully lyrical in all church music. When the final section is ushered in with soprano solo marked 'dolce ed ardente' (sweetly and ardently), the whole panoply of Howells's refined, passionate and wholly indi-vidual style is unleashed on an unsuspecting world. This anthem, whose text is all about longing, gives Howells the perfect opportu-nity to brew his heady mixture of spirituality and sensuality. He comes closer here than in many other such pieces to crossing the line in favour of the sensual; but so what? The result is a work of out-standing beauty using a language which relies heavily on 'blue' notes and false-relations to add piquancy to its long-drawn phrases. This is really where Howells, snowed up in Cheltenham over that new year period, began his pilgrimage in church music.

The two settings of the evening canticles *Magnificat* and *Nunc Dimittis* written one after the other at this time were for King's Cambridge and Gloucester Cathedral. These two sets, together with those he wrote for St Paul's Cathedral in 1951, mark the high tide of his inspiration in setting these words. He wrote twenty sets of evening canticles in his life, from the early G major setting in 1919 to the 'Dallas' canticles of 1971. Each of these settings tries to look afresh at the words, each has something new to say, but nowhere does he achieve the originality of these three great settings.

Collegium Regale is characterised by gentleness. Howells's approach was clearly stated when he said: "... if I made a setting of the 'Magnificat', the mighty should be put down from their seat without a brute force which would deny this canticle's feminine association. Equally, that in the 'Nunc Dimittis', the tenor's domination should characterize the gentle Simeon. Only the 'Gloria' should raise its voice" (Argo). Howells was absolutely true to his promise; the *Magnificat* opens with upper voices (suitably representing Mary) which sing in an almost recitative-like way at the opening. The altos are scored to enrich the texture at "for behold from henceforth", and the tenors and basses only join at "He hath shewed strength with his arm". The *Gloria*, the opening of which is surely amongst the most ecstatic utterances we possess, does indeed raise its voice in the manner of a true doxology. Impressionism, mood-creation (always an obsession with Howells from the earliest days) is very much a part of the experience, as Barry Rose stated in a broadcast: "The opening of 'Collegium Regale' to me, if I didn't know where it was for, speaks of winter afternoons in a candle lit chapel. He's able to catch the mood of everything" (BBC/Prizeman).

If the *Gloucester canticles* are put alongside, we can see Howells addressing the issues in the text in exactly the same way. The *Magnificat* opens with upper voices, but this time, the trebles are divided into two at "for behold from henceforth", and wind in and out of each other's extended melodic lines. There is much melismatic treatment here which lends a feeling of trance-like ecstasy. Howells is still true to his promise in not overblowing the power of the mighty or the 'shewing of strength', but shows a more extended and impressionistic approach to the second half of this canticle from "He hath filled the hungry with good things" than he had in the *Collegium Regale* setting. The *Gloucester Magnificat* is also more motive-based than the *King's* setting, with the opening treble idea used throughout to bind it together. It is also far more 'ecstatic' in its utterances with big intervals employed in the voice parts followed by passionate melismas ("he hath filled" and "as he promised"), and the whole piece (before the *Gloria*) is wound up by an extraordinary progression through the words "Abraham and his seed for ever". This is really new and intensely moving. Another marvellous touch in this work is the variation in the two Glorias. Based on the same material, Howells achieves his moment of ecstasy where, in the *Gloria* of the *Magnificat*, the tenors and basses rise a perfect fifth to give the trebles the springboard for their own rising fifth which takes them over a spine-tingling top A. In *Gloria* of the *Nunc Dimittis* Howells twists the knife wonderfully at this same moment by giving the basses and tenors a different point of departure (4ths and 3rds over a different organ accompaniment) and the trebles a much longer D to crescendo through before launching skywards for their top A. This is given far greater intensity this second time by a more rhapsodic approach. The ending here is also much more extended and impressionist. The feeling is one of timelessness, or perhaps of time standing still. It is the picture painting of "is now and ever shall be: world without end...".

One further thing needs to be added to this overall picture, the issue of acoustics. Howells had been brought up in Gloucester Cathedral where there is an extremely fluid and lively reverberation which colours all the music performed there. It has a decay time of some five or six seconds and is one of the most acoustically perfect buildings in England in which to hear church music. Howells was thus fully aware of the significance of church acoustics, the difficulties they posed for clarity, the great dramatic effects possible by leaving walls of sound hanging in the air, and most importantly, the general feeling almost of levitation when music heard in the Gloucester type of ambience is in the air. Howells knew and understood all this instinctively. It is thus no mere flight of fancy that nearly all his canticle settings are written with particular places in mind. This goes way beyond an affectionate greeting to the incumbent organist and his choir. It is a statement of understanding about the sort of music Howells felt would sound well in that particular building. One only has to look at the next setting he made, for New College Oxford in 1949, to see the point made with the utmost clarity. New College chapel, a great medieval building dating from 1379, was nevertheless roofed in wood and thus the acoustic is comparatively dry; almost completely so, when compared with Gloucester or King's. Thus Howells makes a setting which has much less of the impressionist flavour of the two earlier settings. It still has its moments of ecstasy – "He remembering his mercy" to "Abraham and his seed for ever" is as spine-tingling as anything in *Gloucester* and *King's* – but the heart of the matter is the totally different feeling engendered by knowing that this music would not be heard at least on its home ground in a 'levitational' acoustic. Lest this seem fanciful speculation, it should added that Howells made a note for his setting of the *St Paul's Service* (1951) which explains precisely his approach.

> With the great spaces of St Paul's in mind, as well as the acoustical problems Dr John Dykes Bower had experienced during our training at Gloucester Cathedral, the nature of this setting would be acutely influenced. Prolonged 'echo', notable in St Paul's, would dictate a less rapidly-changing harmonic rhythm than would be feasible in many less reverberant buildings. So it is that in this setting harmonic and tonality changes are deployed in more leisured, more spacious ways. Climaxes are built more slowly. But with these conditions there goes a heightened volume of sound, and a tonal opulence commensurate with a vast church.
>
> (Argo)

So much for the technique in actually writing the work for a particular building, but Howells also said:

> I have never been able to compose a note of music without either a place or a building in my mind. I was commissioned to write a work for St Alban's Cathedral. But I didn't tell the Dean that one day I, as it were, sneaked into the Cathedral at St Alban's because I hadn't been in it for nearly 50 years. And there I sat hoping that no-one would recognise the chap who was going to write some music for them and who wanted to hear the choir, but more than that, I wanted to hear what it felt like – the feeling of that room in which something of mine was going to be sung.
>
> (BBC/Prizeman)

As a postscript to this, something which Robert Bridges wrote would seem to underscore everything Howells achieves in this field:

> If we consider what sort of music we should want to hear on entering a church we should surely, in describing our ideal, say first of all that it must be something different from what is heard elsewhere; that it should be a sacred music devoted to its purpose, a music whose peace should still passion; whose dignity should strengthen our faith; whose unquestioned beauty should find a home in our hearts to cheer us in life and death. What a powerful good such music would have.
> (BBC/Prizeman)

1945 was a memorable year as much for the end of hostilities as anything. The war, of course, had brought with it many privations, not least in terms of food rationing. Things which we all now take so much for granted were rare luxuries during that period. An example of Howellsian humour and of an air of celebration when a rarity was enjoyed came on 2 February. Advised that a fresh egg would be part of the birthday 'feast' for bassoon-playing Cambridge friend Hugh Crosthwaite, Howells wrote a *Grace for a Fresh Egg* in the style of a Minuet, and forever blessed the day!

On 14 February Howells was deeply saddened by the death of his old friend, the artist Sir William Rothenstein who died at his home, Far Oakridge, where Howells had been such a frequent visitor over the years. A memorial service followed on 6 March. Later that same week Howells was back in Cambridge and noting "an incredibly lovely day – crocuses on the Backs". More significant deaths were to follow with David Lloyd George dying on 6 March, and President Roosevelt on the anniversary of Michael's birth, the day he would have been nineteen years old. More significant still, however, was the memo note Howells made for the week of 29 May: "All this week German army disintegrating. Capitulation of German West Armies at Luneberg 6.10 p.m. Friday". Then, bluntly, on Tuesday the eighth, "Victory Day – Churchill's declaration 3 p.m.". He and Dorothy went to Buckingham Palace to see the King, Queen and Churchill wave to the crowds from the balcony at 2.20 p.m. As a postscript to this terrible time, Howells noted that Himmler killed himself when he was captured at Luneberg on Thursday evening the twenty-fourth.

Life seemed to be being lived at a quite frantic pace as he dashed from Cambridge to London, to Birmingham, Edinburgh and Glasgow, where it seems he had an illicit meeting recorded in the kind of code he used: "Early shoes. Tea-carrying up Sahara. Into Teviot Place with Herbert and J. Back to Ness. Then X again...". He went straight on to Brighton, Bristol, and back to Edinburgh, where there were daily assignations with 'Sahara' or 'X'.

On Sunday 16 September he finished the *Six Pieces for Organ* with the *Saraband in Modo Elegiaco*. The whole set of pieces had taken six years to complete and represents Howells at his most wide-ranging and original in terms of the organ. This *Saraband*, for instance, is certainly a stately dance modelled on Elizabethan examples, but with a wholly contemporary and remarkably menacing air about it. It presents a particularly unusual procedure for Howells as it begins softly, with the heavy second-beat accents (the characteristic of the Saraband) giving it something a lopsided feel. The gravity of the piece takes this in its stride, however, actually giving it weight and substance. As its breathtaking intensity builds phrase by phrase, so does the volume, until the final line of music positively cries out for some sort of release. No crescendo/climax/diminuendo piece this, but a disturbing cri-de-coeur. Whether this was occasioned by another Michael anniversary noted ten days earlier ("10th anniversary of Mick's death"), or anger at the carnage and waste of yet another world conflict, albeit now at an end, we will never know.

On 9 December he notes his "last day at St John's" and that he entertained various students, including John Margetson, before setting to work on some more organ pieces urgently required by the BBC. Sir John Margetson recalls this final contact with Howells at St John's:

> On his last night in College about three or four of us went to his rooms after dinner [actually noted in Howells's diary as Hugo; Dolf; Margetson; Brittles and Ellison] and, as was our custom, settled down to talk well into the night. But on this occasion, about midnight, Herbert said he would have to throw us out. He had promised some time back to write some short organ voluntaries for the BBC. They were long overdue and he had to deliver them to the BBC the following week. He gave us all farewell gifts – mine was his copy of Hugh Spencer Dyke's 'Petron', which I

have always loved and carried with me all round the world....
With these gifts in our hands we left Herbert to his work. The
following morning I walked into First Court and heard a
tremendous noise emanating from the Chapel. I went into the
Chapel and met Herbert descending from the organ loft. He
looked very pleased with himself. He told me that he had completed the pieces and had just played them through. He then
gave me the first draft manuscripts as a momento of his last
night in St John's.

(JM/CR)

And so he came to the end of a far more important stretch of time
for him than he might possibly have anticipated when he was asked
to stand in for Robin Orr four years earlier. What was set in motion
during this period set the pattern for his creative work for the rest of
his life.

NINE
Coronations and Commissions

On 5 January 1946 Howells travelled to Lydney to be with his mother who was failing fast. He noted in his diary that he was working on the F sharp *Magnificat* and *Nunc Dimittis*, which must be the canticles for the *Collegiate Church of St Peter in Westminster* although they are publicly dated 1957. Indeed there is a diary entry for 24 February that year noting that he worked on the composition that day, and that he gave Sir William McKie the manuscript on the following Thursday. It would seem, however, as this is his only set of canticles in F sharp and he notes it only by key at the 1946 stage, that he wrote it then and simply revised it for McKie when the subject of a 'Westminster Abbey' service came up. The next day, 6 January, he has "a lovely long day with mother. The F sharp Magn. and Nunc finished while talking to her". 24 January Thursday: "Went to Lydney to mother's bedside"; 25 January Friday: "With mother. Spoke to her for last time at 10.20 tonight"; 26 January Saturday: "She slept from 2 a.m. Mother died at 9.30 tonight. She was 90 but for 3 or 4 months."

Elizabeth Howells had outlived her husband by twenty-seven years. Always a tower of strength to her youngest son, she nursed him through his serious illness and convalescence at the end of his student days and was always on hand to welcome him and his family whenever they were able to return to Lydney which, despite unhappy childhood memories, they did regularly. Still on the domestic front, another important event occurred just a month later

142

on 23 March, when Herbert and Dorothy made their final house move just down the road in Barnes. As Howells noted: "Home now at 3 Beverley Close. Slept there tonight." This move was accomplished partly with the financial help of Lady Olga Montagu, Howells's long-time patron and friend, and this was the house which occasioned Howells being able to put at the end of all his future compositions: "3:BC", causing raised eyebrows from small boys and curious adults alike.

Between August and December Howells was at work on a *Sonata for Clarinet and Piano* which he was writing for Frederick Thurston, the finest British clarinettist of his time. He must have finished the work over Christmas, which was usually a fruitful time for him, as his diary entry for New Year's Day 1947 records that he was "Clarinet Sonata copying". Soon afterwards, on 27 January, the work received its first performance in a broadcast on the BBC's Third Programme with Eric Harrison playing the piano.

As we saw in the last chapter, the success of the *Clarinet Sonata* was partly due to his addressing the problems he faced with the *Oboe Sonata*. Burying that work with scant ceremony, he picked up similar threads in this new work, and made the four-movement scheme of the older *Sonata* into a streamlined two-movement structure here. It is a big, rhapsodic work which reveals a deep love and understanding of the instrument. The clarinet, which of all the woodwind instruments is closest to the human voice, is capable of such a huge range of both pitch and dynamic that it suited Howells's purposes admirably, and was far better adapted to coping with the gruelling demands placed on the clarinettist than the *Oboe Sonata* had been for that instrument. Howells originally wrote the Sonata for the A clarinet, but when it was published it had been changed to the more commonly used B flat instrument which rendered the lowest C sharp which Howells had included unavailable.

The *Sonata* was well received at the time, and a contemporary critic described it as "brilliantly written for both instruments" and "original in form" (MT 1.56). The critic continued: "Howells succeeds in using this now rather too familiar device (3+3+2 quaver rhythm in a 4/4 bar), like the rather luscious and no longer quite modern harmonies in which he delights, with such extraordinary skill, invention and taste that he makes out of them something that is still very fresh, attractive and spontaneous, rather like (but not too much like) Walton in flavour, almost as buoyant in melody, and with the same rhythmic springiness" (ibid).

The diary notes that 12 April 1947 "wd have been Michael's 21st birthday". Five days later Howells was at Lambeth Palace to support his old friend Herbert Sumsion who was being given an honorary doctorate (Cantuar) by Archbishop Fisher in recognition of his services to church music. Two months later, 1 June, Ursula was married to Davy Dodd, an event which gave Herbert and Dorothy great happiness. Howells got on very well indeed with Ursula's new husband to begin with, and used to meet him frequently for lunch or tea. Sadly the marriage was only to last a few years. Later on, in September, he was back in Gloucester conducting his *Elegy* at the festival just the day after Sir Walter Alcock, his great mentor who all those years before had appointed Howells as his first assistant at Salisbury Cathedral, had died.

This was to be a difficult time for Howells, as Dorothy had to go to St Mary's Hospital to have an operation on 19 September. In the next three weeks he notes "D pretty ill", "D worse again", "D very ill". In the middle of all this, on 8 October he wrote: "V-W with me at RCM 4-5.30 shewing me new Parry motet". This is Vaughan Williams's *Prayer to the Father of Heaven*, a most moving tribute to his old friend. Finally, on Tuesday 14 October, Howells recorded: "D's great change for better". The feeling of relief is almost palpable.

Exactly a month later, on 14 November, Princess Elizabeth gave birth to Charles, her first child. In honour of this imminent event Howells had been commissioned by the BBC to write a work for orchestra. In the event he decided to look back at his early Suite: *The Bs* and rework the *Scherzo* ('Blissy') and the *Mazurka* alias *Minuet* ('Bunny'). He repackaged the two movements under the collective title 'Music for a Prince' – presumably 'Music for a Princess' had things turned out differently – and the work was broadcast at 6.15 p.m. on the Third Programme the day after the birth. It was then performed a couple of months later at a Promenade Concert in the Royal Albert Hall conducted by Sir Malcolm Sargent on Saturday 22 January. Herbert and Dorothy spent the day up in London, lunching with Sargent and having tea with Ursula before attending the concert in the evening. When they returned home afterwards they were horrified to discover that their house had been burgled. Dorothy always secured the house well, including locking interior doors. But they found that two doors had been knocked down, and that the family silver had been taken including valuable Georgian cutlery. The thieves must have been disturbed in their work, as some articles were found later on Barnes Common where they had obviously been dropped in their rush to escape. As with all such infringements of privacy, it was a deeply disturbing event for the family.

The fact that Howells had recycled a previous (and much earlier) orchestral work to make *Music for a Prince* rather than taking the opportunity to write a wholly new work for this important celebration is indicative of his attitude to composition at this stage of his life. It is almost certain that he felt that a new orchestral work would suffer the same fate as all the rest of his music in that medium, and that people in the concert hall of 1948 were really not interested in the style of music which he had to offer them. It is likely that this new-old work, which he liked, said as much of what he had to say in this genre as anything new he could compose. With his mind full of smaller scale keyboard pieces and music for the church, orchestral music was not part of his current scheme of things.

The event towards which everything had been moving since Michael's death fourteen years earlier was to take centre stage on 30 August. Almost no one knew of the existence of *Hymnus Paradisi* which had been completed in short score and put in a bottom drawer as a personal document. As is by now obvious, Howells's son was ever-present for him, and no anniversary of birth or death passed without a diary remembrance, or very often a visit to Twigworth. Tuesday 23 April 1949 was no exception when "Michael's 23rd birthday" was recorded. However deep the wound, though, time had passed – a considerable amount of time – and when Herbert Sumsion asked Howells if he might have anything new which the forthcoming Gloucester Festival (1950) might perform, Howells decided that perhaps the time was right to bring this long-buried work to life. On Tuesday 30 August he played *Hymnus* to Sumsion and then left the score with him for further perusal. Sumsion took it to Ashmansworth to show Finzi who wrote to Howells in admiration saying "It's exciting to know that we shall be hearing it at Gloucester next Sept." Things seem to have thus been decided, especially when Sumsion confirmed arrangements by writing "to say definitely that I want to do it at next year's Festival". For whatever reason, the order of events in later years became muddled, and Howells said that it was Vaughan Williams who had persuaded him to have it performed. Certainly he had asked both RVW and Boult for their opinions *after* Sumsion and Finzi had seen the work and expressed their enthusiasm. They were equally enthusiastic, but this served only to confirm to Howells that the work should now have a public performance.

Time was now of the essence as Sumsion had requested vocal scores by the beginning of April (also asking for a piano reduction which might be simplified 'to facilitate rehearsals') and these had to be taken to Novello's for engraving. The whole work now had also to be orchestrated, and various diary entries from the beginning of 1950 show him hard at work on this laborious task, whilst also correcting the proofs of material already delivered to the publishers. Then, in August, the rehearsals began with soloists Isobel Baillie and William Herbert, and with the chorus and orchestra.

On 6 September 1950 Howells noted: "15th anniversary of Michael's death. 'St Matthew Passion'. Guildhall luncheon. RVW's new work (piano: choir: orch) (the Fantasia on the Old 104th) in evening. Gale and rain!" Then, the next day: "Early service (cathedral) with Ursula – conducted 'Hymnus Paradisi' at 11.25-12.12 a.m.... Dorothy, Ursula and Davy there". And so *Hymnus Paradisi* came to life, and to unanimous critical acclaim. Of many words written about the work following that performance (and subsequent ones at Worcester and Hereford in the following years), an article in *Music and Letters* (July 1952) by the conductor Reginald Jacques serves to speak for most:

> I shall never forget its impact upon me at first hearing.... I attended the performance to determine the suitability of the work for inclusion in the Bach Choir's programmes. On all other similar occasions, despite firm resolutions, so often made and so

often broken, it has been impossible, even while the music was going on, to prevent one's mind from busily weighing up the pros and cons of possible rehearsals and performance. Would the choir like to study the work? Should I enjoy conducting it? How long would it take in rehearsal and what other music would best support it in a future programme? No such questions, on this occasion, even occurred to me. From the first solemn announcement of the opening theme to its reappearance at the very end when it rises to catch a gleam of light before fading into silence, Herbert Howells's work took complete possession of me; for days afterwards I could think of little else, and I knew no peace until I had mastered its complexities.

Frank Howes, reviewing the work in *The Times* said:

> he... attains a vision, not so much of peace as of light. He starts from the text *lux perpetua,* and the quality of the light changes with the text drawn from half-a-dozen sources. It is nowhere the soft light of the Elysian Fields that Fauré caught from Gluck and put into his *Requiem*. It is the blaze of a thousand suns in the 'Sanctus'; it is a golden radiance in the penultimate chorus; and at last to the words *requiem sempiternam* it is the light of the dawn.

Gerald Finzi wrote memorably in the *Musical Times* (April 1954) about the phenomenon of *Hymnu*s when he said:

> Quiller-Couch has written of those springs and streams which dive into chasms and are lost to emerge into daylight at long distances having pierced their way through subterranean channels. This might well describe the impact which 'Hymnus Paradisi' first made on many of its hearers. It was quite clear that the work over-topped such known things of Howells's as had recently preceded it; but a generation had passed since Howells's stream had first dived underground, and it was not easy to remember that behind 'Hymnus Paradisi' lay nearly forty years of creative work.

Such was a contemporary view, and one from a man whose finger was very much on the button of current activity in the world of music in Britain. It therefore places in the context of 'public consciousness' all the works which have been under discussion over the last fifteen years or so of his life, and underlines the fact that Howells, whilst always writing, was not in the public's mind as a composer in the same way as others of his generation because he did not seek performances of his music. Others had to do it for him. In the case of his church music promotion was not necessary as everyone was falling over themselves to secure the next dedication. It is therefore no wonder that Howells expended so much energy on this area of his work. Here, at last, was something which people really wanted – and it mattered very much to him, in the same way that indifference to whole swathes of the rest of his output was really a form of defence and another instance of insecurity.

A biographical index of all the principal musicians working in Britain compiled by Russell Palmer in 1947 makes fascinating reading, especially in what he writes about Howells. The end of the entry reads: "Had he not plunged so deeply into the energetic pursuits of musical adjudication, he would have been one of our foremost music critics today. As it is, his broadcast talks show an extraordinary perception and faculty for probing a work to its very foundations. He is respected as a composer of music for the choir" (BM p.129). So there we have it even more bluntly stated. Composition barely comes into the equation here, and when it is finally mentioned, it gets a brush-off.

In the meantime, Howells was enjoying success undreamt of. Performances of *Hymnus Paradisi* sprung up everywhere: 18 April at a Royal Philharmonic concert; 10 August at the Cambridge Festival; on the anniversary of Michael's death, 6 September, at the Worcester Festival; 10 November at Southwark; 14 November at Leeds; 1 December at the Albert Hall with the Royal Choral Society; and on 12 February 1952 again at the Royal Albert Hall with Jacques conducting the Bach Choir as he had so hoped to do. Other performances followed with great regularity, confirming the work as one of the great choral masterpieces of the century.

The week after the premiere of *Hymnus Paradisi* Howells was once again at work on a choral piece, this time a short work for Christmas called *Long, Long Ago*. As so often, it was composed on a single day, Monday 11 September. It was followed less than a week later by a companion piece *Walking in the Snow*. Both these pieces set poems by John Buxton who wrote them as a prisoner of war in 1940. Very strangely for Howells, who was usually so sensitive to every nuance in a text, *Walking in the Snow* combines two poems by accident which, although compatible, lead to a rather odd non-sequitur. The first poem says: "And there was silence: no voice spoke there, no bird in the branches... and I was alone again, With no one there to know Where my last step was planted..." and then, all of a sudden a lovely girl appears as if by magic: "Oh! Let the snowflakes nestle So lightly in your hair As if the wind had won you Jewels from the air..." and so on in like vein. Knowing Howells, he will have found the second poem so beguiling with its lovely descriptions of female beauty and adornment, that he simply could not stop himself from setting it to music. And who cares anyway, when there is music of the magic of the final phrase which says: "And let your hair go flying About your cheeks and eyes To veil them so a moment, Then again surprise With all the sudden beauty of your uncovered eyes"? Under these conditions, Howells the arch-mystic becomes unashamedly Howells the arch-romantic.

The arch-romantic was also very obviously being nurtured at this time in a liaison with Joan Chissell, critic of *The Times* from 1947, lecturer and broadcaster. Howells's diary is littered with coded assignations referring to 'Chis' ('Chislunch'; 'RunnerChis'; 'ChisKew'; 'Chis-Kew-Chis'); and on one obviously memorable day simply "Haymaking" 6 p.m. on 16 July 1950.

Howells's next set of evening canticles was finished on 26 December 1950 whilst at home in Barnes. This was the *St Paul's Service* with its specialised approach for the extraordinary acoustic already discussed in Chapter 8. Following hard on the heels of the new year, Howells was entertaining Olga Montagu to tea in Barnes little realising how illness was so soon to carry away one of his closest friends and mentors. The same week he sent in the score of the *Kent Yeoman's Wooing Song* to Novello. Composed back in 1933 even before *Hymnus Paradisi*, this work had to wait until 1953, a full twenty years after its conception to see the light of day in a performance. In the meantime Ursula's burgeoning acting career had been given a boost by an invitation to play in New York on Broadway. Both parents proudly record the invitation in their diaries. Dorothy writes on 9 February 1951: "Ursula accepted New York offer". Then, two days later: "Bobs flew to New York. 8 p.m. Anxious to hear if she arrived safely". Herbert recorded that he had "said 'Au revoir' to Ursula". Dorothy adds on the twelfth: "Waiting anxiously for news of Bobs"; and then on Tuesday the thirteenth: "Heard Bobs arrived New York 10 hours late, had to land at Gander owing to ice blizzard". A month later, on Wednesday 14 March: "Ursula opened on Broadway. N.Y." A very proud moment for actress and parents.

On 22 June Howells was at the Royal Festival Hall for the first time having spent the morning at the new South Bank adjudicating performances of his *A Maid Peerless* for women's voices and piano. This was the Ladies' Choir finals in the British Federation of Music Festivals National Festival which was all part of the Festival of Britain taking place at this time. This beautiful small-scale work was another piece which he reworked from an earlier version with small orchestra and completed twenty years before. In his adjudication notes on the various performances he shows clearly that he understands the technical problems with which he faces the choirs both with regard to intonation and interpretation. His comment on the obviously victorious choir from Plymouth is particularly telling: "Superb surrender to the whole nature of the piece" (CPC p.420). It is the use of the word 'surrender' which gives so much away and is also so indicative of his passionate feelings in writing the music. There are echoes here of that previously quoted statement from Hilary Macnamara that he was "amazingly passionate in his response to just about every aspect of life".

Howells heard his *Collegium Regale Te Deum* for the first time on 29 July 1951 at a service at St Michael's Cornhill where his old friend Harold Darke was organist. The following Friday the distressing news reached him via a letter from Lord Sandwich of his sister, Olga Montagu's, illness. Howells immediately wrote to her, but it was a letter she was never to receive as she died at 7 a.m. the following day, Howells's thirty-first wedding anniversary. Howells sat down to write a set of evening canticles for Worcester Cathedral over those two days and completed them by the end of Saturday. Whilst no written dedication offers proof that these pieces were a tribute to her memory, Howells would have had her on his mind all this time, remembering her kindness and the strength of her personality now lost to him. The following week perhaps provided an opportunity to couple her name with that of his own son in a performance of *Hymnus Paradisi* which Howells conducted in the Guildhall at Cambridge on 10 August. The previous day had given him the first opportunity to hear his anthem *Like as the Hart*, performed at St John's, surely a nostalgic occasion for him.

In 1951-52 Howells was President of the Incorporated Society of Musicians and on New Year's Day 1952 he travelled to Malvern for the ISM's annual conference based at the Abbey Hotel, that fine ivy-clad building nestling in the lee of the hills. That first evening he hosted the President's Reception at the Winter Gardens and attended a concert which included his *Piano Quartet in a minor*. The next day he gave his Presidential Address to the conference and he then spent the next three days in and out of meetings, lectures and concerts. Speakers included Cecil Day Lewis, Max Newman, Anthony Lewis and Sir George Dyson; music was performed by Julian Bream and Margaret Ritchie; the Aeolian String Quartet with Leon Goossens; Robert Masters' (piano) Quartet; George Thalben-Ball; and Denis Matthews to whose recital Howells apparently contributed. He left early the next morning in the company of his old student RCM friend Douglas Fox, the legendary organist at Clifton College Bristol, who had lost an arm in the first war but who continued to play as if he had two. In 1977 Howells was to write a tribute piece for organ based on the St Louis of France melody which he had used back in 1941 in the *Folk Tune Set* for orchestra. This was in a set of pieces written by friends and pupils collectively called *Garland for DGAF*.

Perhaps the most far-reaching event early in 1952 was the death of King George VI on Wednesday 6 February. His funeral took place at Windsor on the Friday of the next week and Howells listened to it on the radio. In April it was announced that Sir Ernest Bullock, organist of Westminster Abbey, was to be the next director of the Royal College of Music in succession to Sir George Dyson. That was on 10 April. The next day Howells was once again working on his elusive *Cello Concerto* as the twenty-sixth anniversary of Michael's birth approached the following day. He was working to try to complete the Finale, but yet again without success. Success was less elusive, however, with his continuing work on *Howells's Clavichord*. Having given his mind to further pieces over a three-day period 29-31 July, he composed *Ralph's Fugue* (not one of the pair of pieces which eventually bore the RVW dedication). *Berkeley's Hunt, Bliss's Ballet*, and *Newman's Flight* all followed swiftly, and a considerable amount of time was devoted to the work over the next four weeks leading up to the Three Choirs Festival (Hereford), where *Hymnus Paradisi* was to be performed on Monday 8 September.

On 27 September, three days before the centenary of Sir Charles Stanford, Howells was given his old teacher's signet ring. As Palmer pointed out, this was no ordinary ring: "It originally belonged to a French nobleman (Prince Philippe 'Egalité') who died on the guillotine during the French Revolution. He placed it on the finger of his little daughter, who fled to safety in Ireland. Through three generations of daughters the ring finally came into the possession of Stanford's uncle; Stanford himself wore it for more than fifty years, and Guy Stanford (the composer's son) placed it on Howells's finger at the Memorial service in Westminster Abbey on what would have been Stanford's hundredth birthday. Vaughan Williams and Howells had both been invited to lay a wreath on Stanford's grave in the Abbey, which lies next to Purcell's" (CPC pp.51-52). Ursula now wears the ring.

One week after the centenary Howells was honouring Vaughan Williams at an ISM dinner given to celebrate RVW's eightieth birthday which fell on 12 October. As President of the ISM it was his place to give a speech about his old friend, and who more appropriate could there have been than Howells to speak about Vaughan Williams, when they had been such close friends since that auspicious first meeting in Gloucester Cathedral in September 1910? It was also appropriate because Howells spoke so beautifully; he had such a command of the English language and always drew warm approval from those listening. Reading the text of this particular speech one is struck by his technique of false modesty, flattery of those listening, self-deprecation and a very genuine and moving tribute, when the meat of the speech is eventually reached. It is the line of 'all of you here are really better qualified than I to speak on this occasion, but because I am President, it falls to me...'. It is the line which lists most of the distinguished composers present and ends the list by saying "and at least one other" – well, who? – Oh!, but of course, HH himself! This is a clever technique as it concentrates the minds of the listener in a much more focused way on the missing name than if it had been mentioned. Further self-deprecation comes a few minutes later when he says: "By circumstance of Time and Place I ought to be making what is called an 'after-dinner speech'. I ought to be exercising a wit I don't possess upon the evidence that doesn't exist...." He then goes on to be witty and give that very evidence. There follows a remarkable summing up of RVW's achievements to date. He concludes with a clever discourse on the subject of time and age: "And now, by the ridiculous reckoning of Somerset House, he is said to be 80. There is no rhyme or reason in this convention of a man's age. Titian was still at his mighty creative business at 97. Keats closed his book at 26. Verdi had a mind for newer and greater work at 86: Schubert's work was finished at 31. It would be enchanting to overhear Gladstone and the Younger Pitt discussing – in Elysian Fields – the respective merits of Premiership at 80 or at 24. There is no merit in Somerset House records other than one: that it has given us this blessed opportunity and privilege of honouring a composer who has so deeply enriched our lives" (CPC p.301).

At the start of 1953 Howells was nursing a septic foot which prevented him from travelling to Edinburgh to attend the wedding of the Earl of Dalkeith to Jane McNeill for which he had written an organ piece, the *Siciliano for a High Ceremony* composed on the previous 14 December. This did, however, give him time to fair copy the introit he had been commissioned to write for the forthcoming Coronation of Queen Elizabeth which he had written on Christmas Day. This was *Behold, O God our Defender*. In many ways this short piece sums up succinctly everything which Howells had come to achieve in the short time that he had been writing seriously for the church. The first section, with its calls to "Behold!", as if just gently nudging God to into looking this way, are also full of expectation: the low, quiet start, the rising octave with crescendo for the second, and the ecstatic melismas of the third rising to fortissimo with contrapuntal intricacy leading to a unison end to the phrase for emphasis; all is classic, passionate Howells. But that is just the first phrase. He is asking for God's attention – but why?: to "look upon the face of thine Anointed". So, the first phrase, as passionate as it is, is just a roll of drums, where the second achieves one of the great coup-de-grâces in church music. At the climax of the phrase he reaches C sharp minor in preparation for A major for what is apparently the climactic moment on the second syllable of 'anointed', but it is not. The great moment is given to a heart-stopping resolution in C *major,* of all places, and a whole bar later, from which he travels back to A major for the end of the phrase, at which point we thank God for seat belts! The second half of this remarkable tour-de-force is a rhapsodic meditation with much dividing of parts to enrich the texture. It is Howells at his most sensuous and mystical. The rising phrase towards the word 'better' in "for one day in Thy courts is better than a thousand" is another of those great moments of un-diluted passion where the trebles and tenors split to high As and F sharps respectively before winding down to the end. What a way to start one of the great celebrations in church, and who better to create the right atmosphere for the thousands of onlookers that day, and for the woman at the centre of everyone's attention?

Still on the subject of the coronation, Howells had been commissioned by the Arts Council to contribute a choral work for a *Garland for the Queen.* Ten of the principal composers of the day were asked including Vaughan Williams, Bliss, Finzi, Tippett, Britten and Ireland. Howells's contribution was a setting of a poem by Walter de la Mare called *Inheritance.* De la Mare had apparently written his poem called 'Oh Lovely England' earlier and had not much liked it, saying "it was waiting for YOU", when he saw Howells's setting. Howells evidently gave the piece the name *Inheritance.*

Set for double choir, it takes advantage of its secular setting to let down the barriers which his church music lightly erects around the arena of passion. This is a paean of praise in honour of the country he loved so deeply, and which gave him such creative inspiration throughout his life. It is also given wing by the poet with whose work he so completely identified. For all that, and with lovely things in amongst, this is an example of misjudged vocal textures.

Unrestrained as it is, the effect is of muddiness, especially in the first six pages. If we did not know better, it would be reasonable to assume that the music had been written at the piano, for there the chording sounds wonderful. Translate this into the arena of voices, however, and the extremely lavish harmony, the love of splitting parts up and creating spacious chordal effects while still spinning counterpoint, makes the listener sometimes long for a plain common chord. The middle section, thinner and more urgent, is a relief from the complexity of texture. It is not to say that this music cannot be made to work, and to work well, but the number of choirs capable of achieving this feat are few in number and are brave indeed. There are times when Howells's longing is simply too great, and his desire to wear his heart on his musical sleeve leads him to overreach what is generally achievable by most choirs. Hilary Macnamara's continued assessment of his inner self is revealing: "His public persona covered that (his passion), it was a relatively cool, urbane, debonair, very English personality; and deep down there was an absolutely boiling cauldron of Celtic temperament and passion and despair and exultation – you name it – it was a kaleidoscope which was turning all the time and shifting in balance" (BBC/Green). Perhaps he was influenced, at least in his approach, by the performance of Wagner's *Tristan and Isolde* which he had been to see at Covent Garden the night before completing the piece. Who knows?

This period was tremendously busy for Howells. The *Kent Yeoman's Wooing Song* was at proof stage, along with the Coronation introit and the *St Paul's Service*, which meant that Howells was constantly at Novello's checking the music as it came off the presses. Soon after this he was adjudicating in Kendal when, after a 'children's day' of thirteen hours listening on the inauspicious Friday 13 May 1953, he rang Dorothy at 11 p.m. to discover that the post had brought a letter from the Prime Minister giving the news that he was to be appointed a CBE in the Coronation Honours list to be published on 1 June (the day before the Coronation). Howells was delighted to be honoured on the same day that Walter de la Mare received the Order of Merit and Britten was made a Companion of Honour. Later that day he was at the Festival Hall for the first performance of *A Garland for the Queen* and sat with Rawsthorne,

Tippett, Bliss and Finzi. Boris Ord conducted his Cambridge Madrigalists and Vaughan Williams conducted his own *Tallis Fantasia*.

On the day itself, Herbert and Dorothy arrived at Westminster Abbey at 7.30 a.m. to be escorted to their seats high up in the south aisle. He sat with the Waltons, Blisses and Gordon Jacob. Afterwards they went to Westminster Hall for a reception before going home. Howells afterwards wrote of "Wonderful scenes: wretched weather". His contact with royalty had not quite ended for the present period, as on 14 July he went to Buckingham Palace with Dorothy and Ursula to receive his CBE from the new Queen. He was back at the RCM that afternoon and spent the whole evening scoring the *Kent Yeoman* whose first performance was set for 10 September.

On 27 and 28 April, before all these celebrations, Howells had been moving between Worcester and Birmingham as he stayed in Worcester with David Willcocks (organist at the cathedral) who was conducting *Hymnus Paradisi* in Birmingham Town Hall on the twenty-eighth. Undoubtedly, discussion that Tuesday morning in Worcester was centred not on *Hymnus* but on the major new choral work Howells had been asked to write for the 1954 Worcester Festival, the *Missa Sabrinensis* or 'Mass of the Severn'. This was going to be a much bigger-scale work than *Hymnus Paradisi* and Howells needed all the time he could muster to compose and orchestrate the work in time for that festival.

The first mention of work on the new Mass comes later in the Summer when, on 3 August (his wedding anniversary) he notes "work on Mass (Gloria)". After this, entries which record time spent composing the work come thick and fast. Work on the 'Credo' starts on 10 August, and he notes on 6 September: "Eighteenth anniversary of beloved Mick's going. A mellow September day. Morning copying 'Kyrie' of Mass. 2.30 with Malcolm S[argent], going thro' 'Kent Yeoman'."

On 10 September the Howells family gathered at the Royal Albert Hall for the premiere of *A Kent Yeoman's Wooing Song* performed by the BBC chorus and orchestra with Elsie Morison (soprano) and Owen Brannigan (bass) conducted by Sargent. On the twenty-fourth he was back at work on the *Credo* of the Mass which he finished, and had copied by 9 December.

During the latter part of 1953 several deaths occurred of people who had meant a great deal to Howells. On 3 October Arnold Bax died. He had been a long time friend and supporter of Howells, and Howells dedicated his lovely part-song *The Summer is Coming* to his memory in 1964. On 8 October Kathleen Ferrier died and Howells attended her memorial in Southwark Cathedral on the twenty-fourth. Two days later Sir Ivor Atkins died. Atkins had been organist at Worcester Cathedral and was therefore well known to Howells through the annual Three Choirs Festivals. He was responsible for bringing Elgar's *Dream of Gerontius* to the festival in 1902, soon after its poor premiere in Birmingham. On 12 December Frederick Thurston died, dedicatee and first performer of Howells's *Clarinet Sonata*, and as if to crown a year of losses, his close friend and lifelong supporter Marion Scott died on 24 December.

Howells had lived for so long in Barnes by this time, that it was not in the least surprising when he was invited to be the first President of the newly-formed Barnes Music Club. Concerts had been given under the auspices of the Barnes Council of Social Service for some time, but the Club was formed after some 'trial' concerts had been promoted "to see if there was a musical audience large enough to form a local music club". All the artists very generously gave their services and the series was judged to be a success. So much so, that the pianist Irene Kohler offered to make the first step towards starting the club. Her inaugural concert was given on 29 September 1953 and the club continues to be successful to the present day. Howells was not only President, but a very active supporter until the end of his life.

January 1954 saw Howells hard at work on the Mass. On New Year's Day he worked on the *Sanctus*; two days later he finished it and the *Osanna*. On the seventh he was sketching the *Benedictus*, and on the tenth writing its *Osanna*. The day after Marion Scott's memorial service (22 January) he was working on the *Agnus Dei*. Then, a week later, he received a letter from the Vice-Chancellor of London University offering him the King Edward Chair of Music. (Both Grove and Palmer give 1950 erroneously as the date for this appointment.) This was public recognition not only of his standing as a renowned academic, but also of his outstanding contribution to the nation's musical life over such a broad spectrum of activities. On 28 February 1949 Sir Stanley Marchant died having been organist of St Paul's Cathedral and King Edward VII Professor of Music at London University since 1937. After his death the university had insufficient funds to make a new appointment straight away, and so the chair was vacant between 1949 and 1954. It was not a full-time appointment, and at the time when Howells was was offered the post simply involved giving a small number of lectures, setting examination questions, attending meetings and so on. (This changed in 1964 when Howells relinquished the post to Thurston Dart, the first full-time Professor of Music).

When a new professor was appointed to a university chair in those days, the Peterborough column in the *Daily Telegraph* would congratulate the new incumbent. On this occasion (Tuesday 9 February) the anonymous columnist said that it was the university which should be congratulated, on securing such a distinguished musician to the post.

Just before the news of his university appointment was released in the papers, Howells had been having misgivings about his *Credo* for the Mass, which caused him grave depression. On the eleventh he began work on a new *Credo*. In the meantime orchestration of the completed movements continued apace with an end of the *Gloria* in sight on "Michael's 28th anniversary". On 1 May disaster almost struck as the full score of the *Credo* was thrown from the train in which he was travelling between Cambridge and London at Harlow. How can such a thing happen? More to the point, how can it happen twice in a lifetime? The first completed version of the *In Gloucestershire* string quartet was similarly lost on a train and was never recovered. This however was potentially far more serious. Fortunately, though, luck was on his side this time, and he went to collect his unusual 'lost property' at Liverpool Street Station the next day.

As mid-July came on with time getting very short, he was once again hard at work scoring the *Agnus Dei*. Then, triumphantly, he writes in his diary on 12 July: "Finished the score of 'Missa

Sabrinensis' (score was begun 21 Febry)". The following Saturday he learnt the happy news that Vaughan Williams's new work *Hodie*, also to be performed at Worcester that September, had been dedicated to him. A touching salutation from an old and dear friend.

Just before rehearsals began on Sunday 22 August Howells began work on one of his most beautiful short choral works *The House of the Mind* for chorus and string orchestra. Far from wanting to 'rest from his labours' he seems buoyed up by the finishing of the immense work of *Sabrinensis*. Rehearsals with the soloists in London, then with the chorus in Worcester, and finally with the orchestra for the first three days of September prepared the work for its premiere on Tuesday 7 September at 8.20 p.m. As at the first performance of *Hymnus Paradisi* Howells conducted the work himself and succeeded, once again, in producing a fine performance.

The *Missa Sabrinensis* had nothing of the immediate impact or success of *Hymnus Paradisi* and undoubtedly people were disappointed that the new work did not overtop it. This is hardly surprising, though. How could a work with the genesis of *Hymnus* be matched again? The mistake people made, and continue to make, is in trying to compare the two works. What is indisputable is the extremely taxing vocal parts which Howells wrote for the chorus. Ursula Howells remembered the first performance: "The *Missa Sabrinensis* ... gave the poor choirs at the Three Choirs Festival terrible headaches. Unfortunately it was the year that those poor rabbits were suffering from myxomatosis, and a member of the choir told me that they were having such a terrible time that they all referred to it as the 'Missa Myxomatosis'!" (BBC/Prizeman). The work's second none-too-complimentary nickname, the Severn Bore, was derived from a more regular natural phenomenon. Sir David Willcocks, who prepared the Worcester contingent of the chorus for that first performance said: "It's challenging because he uses both voices and instruments very well, he understands their capabilities. Some would say that he overestimates their abilities, and many basses in amateur choral societies would say that he consistently writes too high for them. That may be true, but he has always assumed, I think, that the forces that are going to sing his music are very good ones, and I think that he's never said to himself,

'as they're amateurs I have got to make concessions'" (BBC/
Prizeman).

Howells, writing the programme note for the first performance,
states that thematic unity was not one of his concerns. Three themes
do return, but none seeks to bind the movements in this way. He
states: "A relationship deeper than any that thematic identity could
enforce has been sought in terms of character and consistency in the
nature of the music, its terms and its inflections". In other words,
this is the apotheosis of his creation of 'mood' music, the 'complex
mood' discussed in Chapter 3. Howells's intention was also to bring
the chorus into focus much as in *Hymnus Paradisi* by making the
soloists "adorn the contrapuntal texture of the chorus" and so that
"the chorus should dominate". Finally, recognizing that the Latin
title of the work might baffle some listeners, Howells explains that
"The Mass derives its title from the Severn – the river linking the
composer's Gloucestershire birthplace with Worcester, the place of
the work's first performance".

Reviews of that first performance were mixed, as expected. The
specialised review in *Music and Letters* (by B.W.G.R.) puts its finger
on a number of strong pulses:

> Dr Howells has, undoubtedly, developed a strong personal style
> – a style which many may not like, but which most must admire.
> This style flowered in 'Hymnus Paradisi', but the new work
> reaches beyond the earlier one, and in so doing seems to break
> its bounds .... The many cases of simultaneous complex rhythms
> perhaps enter the realm of academicism.... It may be dangerous
> to criticize the use of textual superimposition, it has been done
> before, but for the express purpose of shortening an otherwise
> over-lengthy composition... the passage on p144 *et seq* is a differ-
> ent matter... all have the complete text in the end.... The composer
> makes the greatest possible demands on his singers, both
> soloists and chorus, not merely in that they have some very high
> notes to sing, but also because there are so many cases where
> they have to produce narrow vowel-sounds on very high notes
> .... The orchestral scoring is heavy and offers little relief to the
> contrapuntal complexity of the vocal parts.
> (M&L 1.55)

The report by Scott Goddard in the *Musical Times* was less

focused in its criticism of the music. It responded to the one hearing, rather than extended post-concert study as in the previous case. It said:

> Howells's 'Missa Sabrinensis' was sung by the chorus, who bear all the burden (and a heavy one it is) in this work, with such spirit, application and eager sympathy that it was impossible to believe that they were the same people who the day before had sung Elgar's 'The Apostles'. Where that was tame, rising to a genteel expressiveness, the exacting Howells work was sung with a lively vigour which may have been rough at times but had a proper vitality and strength.... As for the music, a single hearing is not enough to satisfy either curiosity or latent feeling of exhilaration. Howells's lithe, muscular counterpoint is at first a bewilderment to the ear, which must have time to sort things out.
>   (MT 11.53)

The two critics agree that the work is too complex. *The Times* critic also weighed in on this point:

> It is fair criticism of the oratorios ... to point out that their texture is too complex. Kinks and curls in the vocal parts and virtually inaudible melismata in the quasi solo writing of the orchestral counterpoints so complicate the score that problems of balance are acute.

And yet in the next breath he takes the opposite tack:

> Conductors have said that they would like to smooth out some of these clusters of arabesque-like detail. Yet if they did, it is pretty certain that the incandescence would go with them, so that the composer can answer the critic with 'too complex for what?', to which the retort is 'for safety'. A recent performance of the Missa Sabrinensis came to grief because the complexity of texture was not mastered.

After the first performance Howells wrote to Arthur Hutchings saying: "In my comparative old age I feel strangely freer to express myself in music – free of the thousand and one fears and fashions, comparisons and estimates being interminably made by one's contemporaries. There is, in so many of us, a crippling concern with public reaction and the critical opinions of Tom, Dick and Harry. The four walls of one's study cannot shut these out: or is it that one fails to learn how to shut them out till one has one foot in the grave?" Thinking of all Howells's past sensitivities this makes interesting reading indeed.

Criticism of a large-scale work like *Missa Sabrinensis* is a difficult and emotive exercise. On one level, we might ask how to approach a work from one who has proved himself such a master of his subject. Liking and disliking apart, has there yet been a performance of the work which actually *deals* with all the issues raised in constructive criticism? The problems are undeniable. The complexity for which the *Missa Sabrinensis* is criticised is found in the final movement of the *Kent Yeoman's Wooing Song*, where three different strands of activity take place simultaneously. How is sense to be made of that to the listener? – yet the *effect* is tumultuous. Maybe this is what the critics have missed: one cannot discuss Howells's music and omit mood and atmosphere. That has been made abundantly clear throughout this book. So perhaps criticism has tried to fit the work to preconceived notions of music which uses words. When the text is as familiar as the Mass itself, is it vital that every word is heard? Enough clues *will* come through to give the listener his bearings. No, the mood and the colour are everything in this instance. As to the charge of muddy orchestration: yes, Howells likes to use his orchestra richly, but two or three bars, even without the singers present, will identify its composer immediately. Once again, is this not a personal trade-mark we should not write off? Perhaps part of the problem is that none of our choral works gets anything like enough rehearsal time in this country as compared with the continent of Europe. This may have made British musicians the best sight-readers in the world, but at what cost? To have time and space to *care* for this work in rehearsal, and to sort out its complex intricacies, might well surprise those critics who are so keen to denigrate its achievements. What is absolutely certain is that this work is unique and its vision almost apocalyptic. The sadness is that its technical difficulties, however justified, will prevent it ever entering the repertory, so it is unlikely to get the kind of performance it has so far lacked. We must be grateful for Chandos Records' vision in recording the work (generously funded by the RVW Trust), so, for all the imperfections of that performance, some clearer idea can be formed as to its strengths and weaknesses, not just on paper but in sound. For, as many commentators have said, Howells has to be *heard* and not simply *read*.

TEN
Stabat Mater and The Final Years

After an endurance test such as *Missa Sabrinensis* demanded, it is extraordinary that Howells should find the energy to start again on exactly the same words in *An English Mass*, written next for Harold Darke and his St Michael's Singers. Whilst only half the playing time, this is by no means a small-scale Mass. Howells scored it for strings and organ, although it is possible (but obviously less satisfactory) with organ accompaniment alone. In this way, the Mass can be performed liturgically, for which purpose Howells added a setting of the *Sursum Corda*. The work was finished on 21 April 1956 and was given its first performance in St Michael's Cornhill on Monday 4 June and broadcast the following Friday. The Princess Royal was in attendance. Afterwards Howells wrote to Darke: "Now the glorious dust is settling on Monday's gay battlefield one or two duties become clear. The first – that you will be so good as to thank all your singers for me. They were grand: quick to learn the bulk of my strange notes, and inspired in finding better ones when mine didn't fit. I was enchanted. Second – to tell you yourself how grateful we were for your immense zest and sheer endurance. You grew younger under a test that wd have knocked most for six."

On 22 June Walter de la Mare died in the morning aged eighty-three. Howells was deeply saddened by this loss of a dearly loved and respected friend whose work had meant so much to him over so many years. The following Thursday de la Mare was buried at St Paul's Cathedral where, years before, he had been a chorister. Since

1919 Howells had been making settings of de la Mare's poems and considered making a *Garland* of songs as a tribute. Work on this project was extremely sporadic and did not settle into a publishable set during Howells's lifetime. He evidently felt strongly, and not surprisingly, that *King David* should form part of it, but that work was already published. However, after de la Mare's death the project became a major preoccupation, and led to Howells completing eleven songs which have been posthumously published together with *King David*, a negotiation between publishers which would surely have delighted him.

This *Garland* contains some of the most beautiful, haunting songs in Howells's output. In a book of this size and scope important things have had to be glossed over, and numerous works, large and small, ignored or referred to only in passing. Part of my purpose has been to encourage the reader to explore further, and to listen to the many recordings now available, which include fine performances of a large number of Howells's songs including the complete *Garland for de la Mare* and *King David*.

Amid the Celtic reflections in the first song *Wanderers*, are shining images of night time, and a nocturnal vision of distant planets. This will have resonated with Howells from his youth when his father would wake him to see and talk about Saturn, Jupiter and Mars; Venus, Mercury, Uranus and Neptune; those very same stars which de la Mare refers to in his poem. This song from 1958 has a timeless, mesmerising, unhurried progress which underscores the unchanging nature of the universe and our wonder at it. *The Lady Caroline*, which follows it, is one of Howells's classic 'beautiful lady' songs. It has all the grace of a stately dance in triple measure from which one can feel the poise of her head, the measure of her tread, and the heartbeat of the onlooker. The picture-painting in Howells's writing puts a mirror to de la Mare's poem and sees in its reflection the object of his desire in all her perfection. Howells was clearly influenced in his setting by one of the great songs of the Edwardian era, W. Denis Browne's *To Gratiana, Dancing and Singing*. Although Howells's song is entirely personal, the similarities, where they occur, are in the style of left-hand accompaniment with rich basses and the style of their second beat releases. The final moments of this song are the most musically telling where de la Mare says: "The window smouldered keen with frost; Yet still she twisted, sleeked and tossed her beauteous hair about". Howells's imagination places a simply perfect 'frost' chord just after the word has been sung, from which there is a warm resolution to allow the girl to twist, sleek and toss – also 'drawn' in the music – her lovely hair.

Before dawn from 1969 is another powerful, emotional song with endlessly long phrases, timeless pacing and a poem which hovers gently between sacred and secular, allowing Howells some glances over his shoulder at quasi-church-style progressions which add to this song's haunting nature. It is easy to see why he was so drawn to these poems of de la Mare, the imagery so vivid and so concerned with *sound*: "The blackbird and the thrush Pipe but a little as they flit Restless from bush to bush; Even to the robin Gabriel cried softly, 'Hush'...". For someone who listed in the 'recreation' section of his *Who's Who in Music* entry 'Silence', this will have been a potent moment in verse. Howells's creation of the atmosphere of this chilly, dark, silent time before dawn breaks is marvellously transformed at the end of the song to welcome the onset of day in another powerful poetic image: "Yet in this frozen mirk the Dawn breathes, Spring is here!".

The whole set of these songs is balanced between the inward, emotionally powerful ones described above, and livelier, sometimes quasi-comic songs such as *A Queer Story*, which is about three farmers who bet each other a pound that one would dance the other two into the ground; or *Andy Battle* which, despite all its 'yeo ho's' is not really comic at all. Neither Howells nor de la Mare was good at being light-hearted. There was almost always a twist in the tail/tale leading back to serious roots. This absence of light relief is the major problem in Howells's music for the listener generally, and one could gaze at navels for years in search of the psychological reasons behind it. It might be said that it simply was not his way; but his childhood family problems remind us that some people spend their whole lives trying to erase, or at least ease their deeply scored emotional scars. Howells's musical attempts at the light-hearted usually come out like a forced smile, and soon become wearisome. What we value in Howells is his understanding of the deep things of the mind; that he can put a voice to our spirituality, our very sense of being, and in a way almost *too* human, to that deepest of all senses, longing. From this we may, or may not gather comfort, but there is at the very least, a sense of something fundamental shared.

In July 1956 Howells was yet again at work on a Mass setting, this time to complete his series of *Collegium Regale* settings for King's College Cambridge. This work is interesting in so far as it is a rare example of a twentieth-century 'parody' Mass which takes other music as its starting point, in this case his own *Collegium Regale* settings, and builds a new work around it.

In August he sat down, once again, to re-examine his clavichord pieces which, like de la Mare's *Garland* had been stacking up over a long period. As usual, once he decided to get on with something, he stuck at it until it was finished. *Dart's Saraband*, for Thurston Dart, was finished and posted to him the next day, 10 August, and other pieces followed over the coming months until the whole set was finished with a final copy in place on 27 January 1958.

The Gloucester festival that year saw yet another performance of *Hymnus Paradisi* which took place "on the 21st anniversary of beloved Mick's going". Howells noted it as being "superb". Then Gerald Finzi died. This was another infinitely sad moment, at which Howells wrote of "a sorrowful loss to all of us. Dorothy and I saw him for the last time in the cathedral gardens on 8 Sept. He was with Joyce in their brake – just about to set off home. We thought he looked tired. He was cheerful, and full of praise for the festival just ended". The next morning Howells wrote a beautiful tribute to him for his Clavichord collection, *Finzi's Rest*, and dedicated it "For Gerald, on the morrow of 27th September 1956". He actually wrote two pieces with the same title, but chose the published one in preference.

On 20 December the following year Howells became a member of the Savile Club in London, something he was to grow to enjoy and value greatly as time went on, and a lunching facility which became a regular feature of life. Some of the pleasure of that moment was diminished in that Ursula had been taken to hospital in Midhurst on 29 November suffering from tuberculosis. Not suprisingly this affected Howells greatly, and he also missed her company terribly: "Lonely with U away!"; later, when he visited: "with Ursula for nearly 4 hours. Low spirits". Tuberculosis was of course life-threatening, and Howells must have felt that the demons were once again chasing his tail as, having taken his son, they might now also take his daughter. Ursula, however, was as fortunate as her father had been all those years before when he had been a 'guinea-pig' for radium to treat his Graves disease. Drugs to deal with tuberculosis had just been discovered. Ursula's illness lasted until she was released from hospital on 23 October 1958. Howells noted on the twenty-sixth: "Home 6.o'c. Ursula let me in: Laus Deo!". She had been in hospital eleven months.

On 3 July, in the middle of Ursula's incarceration, Howells was saddened by a telephone call from the BBC in Bristol telling him that his old friend and patron Lord Bledisloe had died aged ninety. Far more significant than this, however, was the loss of Vaughan Williams the next month on 26 August. "Beloved RVW died at dawn today... and so here's Holy Day, and the co-relative is in the coda of his 5th Symphony. A quiet day at Barnes, and a day of great beauty – perfectly still". The next day: "Barnes. No power to work. All RVW ...." And on 28 August: "RVW cremated, during a violent morning of thunder. A drab, wet afternoon. Then sheer sunset glory high-placed." Finally, to close the chapter on 19 September: "RVW buried in the Abbey. There with D 11.5 till 1 p.m.... A curious moving, unforgettable day, beautifully concluded".

On 27 January 1959 Howells was elected the third John Collard Life Fellow in succession to Vaughan Williams. What a wonderful feeling of inheritance there must have been for him in this. The passing on of Stanford's signet ring had taken that generation to a perceived new leader in Howells; and now came this honour, given in direct succession to the 'Grand Old Man of English Music'. All was now falling into place as Howells himself reached the autumn of his own life. Four days later he was addressing the Royal College of Organists as their new President.

The real business of the year, however, was still to come, and was to preoccupy him for the next five years. Back in 1954 he had been invited to write a major choral and orchestral work for the Bach Choir of which David Willcocks was now the conductor. It took him a long time to decide on a text for the work. Finally he chose the thirteenth-century poem *Stabat Mater*, set so many times by composers as various as Palestrina, Pergolesi, Haydn, Rossini, Verdi, and, significantly, Howells's old teacher Stanford.

Why did Howells choose to set these introverted, passionate, almost sado-masochistic words at this time? There are numerous reasons and facts which can be pointed to as indicators. One, however, would seem to speak louder than other, perhaps more plausible reasons: he would do it because everything he had been writing throughout his life led to this moment. (He was sixty-seven when he started writing the work in 1959 and seventy-three when it reached its first performance). He *knew* that his unique, idiosyncratic style was the perfect vehicle for mirroring the intense, passionate love and grief which lie at the heart of this poem. He very much admired Stanford's *Stabat Mater* and wrote hotly to *The Times* (in a joint letter with Vaughan Williams) in its defence when it was denounced by a critic. However, admirable as it is, Stanford's work is 'beautiful', and surely, no setting of this text should be beautiful in that sense of the word which implies comfort? Howells's setting lays you on a bed of nails and offers you a knife for good measure, taking you through the whole gamut of emotion before offering an exhausted hope of Paradise at its conclusion.

So much for the numinous. What of the circumstances surrounding its composition? Howells had lived through two World Wars, and many entries in his diaries for those years show him following every twist and turn of events as the horrors unfolded. Judging from diary entries for this period, he is as agitated about current events as he was back in the 1940s, or even in the Great War. The reason was the new nuclear threat, which was literally terrifying.

His preoccupation with developments is clear: 31 August 1961: "Grave bomb-testing news from Russia"; 1 September: "NYO [National Youth Orchestra, on whose Board of Directors Howells served] on way to bomb-exploding Russia.... Mind on Russia"; 2 September: "Mind on Russia"; the week's notes: "A week of blessed sunshine but ruined by Russia"; 9 September: "International stress ... a sort of Hardy setting for possible drama"; and so on. The drama of the Cuban missile crisis the following year, and President

Kennedy's assassination in 1963, with which Howells was so soon to be intimately associated, fuelled his sense of unease. In the background remained the immutable fact of his own son's death which coloured everything he did. It is also fair to say that Howells was an actor and loved to create a crisis out of a drama, and a drama from some often quite insignificant thing. The 'ham' in him loved telling the world of his doings through his diaries. The *Stabat Mater* is a dramatically anguished text, so this was another level on which he could approach it. A different influence in his choice of poem – unusual because visual, not textual – was the *Pietà* sculpted by Michelangelo in St Peter's Rome. This extraordinary work of art shows the dead Christ lying across his mother's knees and cradled in her right arm as she looks down with infinite sadness on his limp, lifeless body. No parent who has lost a child could view that sculpture without a sense of shared loss and of knowing. It seems almost gratuitous to keep on about Michael in this fashion unless one realises that the loss was ever present for Howells too, like a ground bass to his existence. Unrelated to any anniversary, but very much with Ursula and her illness in his mind, Howells wrote on 25 May 1958: "By bus again to see Ursula... the countryside brilliant (as it so often was at most tragic moments in Thos. Hardy's novels!). Wondering what Gloucester and Hereford were like". Then, the next day: "Rain and gloom – but the rain turned away into a sheer beauty of light. Prudentius 'Hymnus circa Exsequias Defuncti' kept my mind in safe refuge – as once it did in Sept 1935 for loss of Mick" – and there he is again.

The *Stabat Mater* was a lengthy project for Howells. He found it difficult to write and encountered many problems with it. The first record of any work on it comes on 26 August 1959. Howells was copying the completed first movement four days later. He began the second movement *Cujus animam gementem* the next day, but could not find its shape. A week later he had given the movement life as a *Saraband* (one of his favourite stylised dances), whose slow, triple measure with second-beat emphases was a perfect setting for Mary's weeping lamentation. Work then ceased for almost a year before picking up again with the fourth movement *Eia Mater*. August seemed to be the time each year when Howells's mind would turn back to the big ongoing task, as it was yet another year before he returned to continue its composition. Perhaps the completion of *A Sequence for St Michael* (no surprises there ...) the day before work resumed on *Stabat Mater* on 1 August 1961, spurred him into renewed action on the project.

This *Sequence* written for the 450th anniversary of the foundation of St John's College Cambridge, which occurred that year, contains Howells's most overt cri-de-coeur in its two opening choral cries of 'Michael', agonisingly harmonised. The text by the eighth-century poet Alcuin is used in Helen Waddell's matchless translation (how often she features too!). The use of this text, and Howells's impressionistic response to it, says almost all that needs to be said about the kind of imagery which inspired him. It is always concerned with the mystical; God in his heaven above, and the people on their knees on earth. Who could fail to be moved by such an image as Helen Waddell, in her genius, conjured from Alcuin's Latin: *"Thou with strong hand didst smite the cruel dragon, And many souls didst rescue from his jaws. Then was there a great silence in heav'n, And a thousand thousand saying 'Glory, to the Lord King'"*? The idea of the totality of that silence, and the gradual murmur of these countless souls uttering their near-silent prayer of praise, is quite overwhelming. Howells treats it with extraordinary skill at the point where 'Glory, to the Lord King' begins, starting almost like a rumour with the basses, and almost immediately bringing in the two-part sopranos, floating, wafting, like drifting incense while the other parts sing in gentle ecstatic melismas. This is Howells at his most persuasive. What a gift to a composer of Howells's sensibility was Helen Waddell when she could offer such imagery, or as elsewhere in this poem, and set by Howells for tenor solo: *"Thou wast seen in the Temple of God, A censer of gold in thy hands, And the smoke of it fragrant with spices Rose up till it came before God"*. It is sad that mystery, as in so many aspects of life, has all but disappeared, and with it (with one or two brave exceptions) the vertical as against the horizontal in our worship.

And so work resumed on *Stabat Mater*, although fitfully, and there were still long periods with none. On 28 December 1961: "Turning to 'S.M.' again after 3 months nothing-done-to-it". August of 1962 again found him "struggling back to 'S.M.' frame-of-mind", and on Christmas Eve that year he telephoned David Willcocks to postpone delivery of the completed work until June 1964. August 1963 did see the completion of the vocal score on the eighteenth, with some final revisions made to the end of the work on the twenty-fourth, but postponement was again necessary as it was not until New Year's Day 1965 that he began work on the scoring. The full score was finished on his seventy-third birthday (17 October) and it was sent to Novello's the next day. Rehearsals began on 15 November and the work came finally to its first performance a week later on 22 November 1965. Robert Tear was the tenor soloist. Howells dedicated the work to "the Bach Choir, and in affectionate memory of Ralph Vaughan Williams".

Writing in *The Guardian* the next day, the critic Hugo Cole displayed considerable sensitivity in dealing with this extraordinary work which, like the *Missa Sabrinensis* cannot have been easy to assess on a single hearing:

> Herbert Howells's 'Stabat Mater'... is a work that achieves homogeneity through concentration of a single emotional mood. For once, thematic content, processes of development and extension, rhetoric and drama, are all of secondary importance. What we respond to is the tone of voice: a tone that conveys grief, but never rebellion; sustained sorrow, but never bitterness.

He goes on to make further highly pertinent points:

> Herbert Howells's own, wholly personal mode of speech owes nothing to the developments and experiments in musical semantics of post-war years. Yet in this context, it has a rightness that is beyond question. The 'Stabat Mater' seems to be one of those works in which the subject has chosen the composer rather than the composer choosing the subject.

The last line there is a deeply perceptive assertion. Given the many criticisms of Howells's orchestration, the scoring of this work is particularly successful. Where the *Missa Sabrinensis* was lavish, this is spare; where that work was thick-textured, this is translucent. This is not to imply that the *Stabat Mater* is not complex. In its way, it is as complex as the *Missa Sabrinensis*, especially in the habitually difficult vocal parts. But its message and thrust is so focused as almost to make light of the pitfalls encountered on the way. The main difference between these two works is that the *Stabat Mater* is a single poem and the work therefore unfolds as a continuous span with the last three movements actually marked *segue*. In the Mass, although unity is achieved by mood, as we have seen, each section inevitably has its own character and an aural double bar at each movement ending. The conception, in other words, is completely different, as is the approach. There is little doubt that the *Stabat Mater* is the greater of these two major choral works. It is absolutely original; it gets completely under the skin of the harrowing poem; it deals with the orchestra versus choir in a far more successful way than in the Mass (however an apologist may try to justify his treatment in that work); the role of the soloist is clearly and passionately defined; and it acts as a proper summation of Howells's life and work. What followed over another thirteen or so years of composing life consisted of a plethora of increasingly irrelevant choral pieces, composed mainly to satisfy the apparently insatiable appetite of organists who wanted the kudos of their own Howells dedication. Certainly there is significant music after *Stabat Mater*, but the long coda which brought his life to its conclusion was soft-pedalled after his great work was really done.

One work composed whilst at work on *Stabat Mater* which has become a classic of twentieth-century choral music, was the result of another tragedy; an event which set the world spinning in the magnitude of its audacity. On Friday 22 November 1963 President Kennedy was assassinated in Dallas, Texas. Shortly afterwards Howells was commissioned to write a motet to be sung at his memorial service (a joint American/Canadian event) in Washington Cathedral. As always, much thought was given to a suitable text, as the diary for Sunday 10 May records: "Search for text for Washington work: Kennedy memorial". By the sixteenth the decision had been made, and again the theme resurfaced from Helen Waddell's inspired translation of Prudentius's 'Hymnus circa Exsequias Defuncti'; those same words which, though not used, featured so powerfully in the early stages of *Hymnus Paradisi*, and which, as we have seen, came back to him at crucial moments in his life. He will have relished the opportunity to use them here, having discarded them from *Hymnus* during the sketches stage. He finished the motet on 18 May and had it ready for the publishers on 6 June. Here, then was another coming full-circle, as all the post-Michael strands in Howells's life sought to converge in a confluence of memories and events. Significant here, however, is that Howells was being asked to write something which would speak on behalf of everyone. This work was, in a sense, the mouthpiece of a generation responding to a tragedy with which Howells could wholly identify. This is why the commission was particularly appropriate, and why the outcome is an undoubted masterpiece. Hilary Macnamara said, tellingly, that Howells "was so deeply affected by the death of Kennedy. It brought again to the surface some of the same feelings of loss. He used that text because it was as if it was a special gift almost to Kennedy that he should use that text. Another thing was, of course, that Herbert was a man of gestures. He had this very theatrical side to his nature, and it was also of the most superficial level, too, a gesture which could be *seen* to be a gesture – the linking of these two (Kennedy with Michael)" (BBC/Green).

On 5 March 1965, Howells learned of Helen Waddell's death at the age of seventy-five. The diary entry calls her a "marvellous woman". But as sad as this was, it was overshadowed by Winston Churchill's death the previous January. Herbert and Dorothy watched the "incredible state funeral" on television which they found "quite unique and deeply moving. Another 'finest hour' for him and for the Nation".

One of Howells's characteristics was his tendency to rush everywhere. He was always running about; it seemed quite natural for his size and trim figure. However, as he grew older, he was also tending to trip and fall rather more. In 1955 he had two very nasty falls in Oxford and Hamilton (Scotland) within a month, but this was nothing compared to what happened to him on Saturday 14 January in 1967. He had arranged to meet his nephew Neil at Mount Vernon Hospital at Northwood where Howells's immediately elder brother Leslie (Neil's father) was undergoing treatment for cancer. Neil had offered to collect him from the RCM but Howells refused this, saying that he had more work to do, and would meet him at the hospital.

Howells left the train, ran for a departing bus, jumped to catch it and missed, falling very heavily and breaking his femur. That it was the wrong bus naturally compounded the irony. Remarkably, he got himself up and onto the correct bus, which took him to the hospital where he managed to get to the casualty ward. Fearing that he might have to stay in this remote hospital for some time whilst he underwent surgery, he asked his nephew to ring a consultant surgeon who lived opposite him in Barnes to ask if he could be transferred immediately to Charing Cross Hospital. From there he would still be able to see his students, and his family would have easier access. This was arranged and he was transferred that very evening by ambulance.

Recovery from such a serious accident was inevitably slow, and when the present author first met Howells as a student at the RCM in 1970, he was still walking unevenly with a stick, although it was not long afterwards that he was able to abandon it. As if all this was not enough, Dorothy then had a small heart attack on the Thursday following his fall. Fortunately it was not serious, but it did mark a growing vulnerability as the pair of them aged.

Ever resilient, and never wanting to waste a moment longer than he had to, he was back with his manuscript paper on 24 February making the first sketches of a *Magnificat* and *Nunc Dimittis* for Winchester Cathedral, and going on to finish it as quickly as ever on 5 March. On 29 August he was at work on another *Magnificat* (probably the *Chichester Service*) the day after he had been to see his elder brother Leonard in St Luke's Hospital in Guildford. "He seemed far away. I felt I would never see him again". On 3 September he remembered Oliver Cromwell's birthday. Throughout his life Howells had an extraordinary memory for dates and anniversaries, and sometimes of the most obscure people. He called it a "life habit". For instance, only a fortnight after his fall he wrote: "Carolus Rex killed 318". He always remembered Bach's birthday, and very often Napoleon's, too, and on 1 May 1969 noted: "200th anniversary of Wellington's birth".

The day after Cromwell's anniversary on 4 September, Leonard died at 5 p.m. That very day Howells "began and finished *A flat Nunc Dimittis* (*St Augustine's Edgbaston*); strange coincidence", by which he meant that the words of the *Nunc Dimittis* begin: "Lord, now lettest now thy servant depart in peace".

The year 1969 was an important one, as what Howells described as his 'Irish Pilgrimage' began in April. This refers to his close friendship with the pianist Hilary Macnamara. The next month he was in St George's Hospital to have a hip replacement and, in another month's time, a prostate operation. He stayed in hospital from 6 to 28 May, returning home to Barnes that day. Work for the rest of that year focussed on the completion of the de la Mare *Garland* (in July, August and September), and on the composition of a *Magnificat* and *Nunc Dimittis* for Hereford, the last of the trio of 'Three Choirs' cathedrals to receive a set of canticles from him.

In June 1970 Edward Heath, the leader of the Conservative Party walked into 10 Downing Street as the country's new Prime Minister following a successful election campaign. This event brought to Howells's mind a promise which he had made to Heath years before when Heath had been organ scholar of Balliol College, Oxford; that if he ever became Prime Minister Howells would write him an organ work. Heath had asked Howells for a reference to present to Ernest Walker, director of music at Balliol, to support his application for the organ scholarship (he was already an undergraduate at the college). Howells had adjudicated Heath conducting the Broadstairs Glee Club when he was only fifteen and had awarded them first prize. Heath therefore felt that Howells might remember him and support him, which he did. On 23 June 1970, just four days after Heath's triumphant entry into Downing Street, Howells wrote to him reminding Heath of the promise, and committing himself to the composition of a new work. In return, Heath invited Howells to a party at Chequers on 9 September and the deal was sealed.

As 1971 dawned, Howells was becoming less enamoured of the labour of writing this organ work which was proving rather elusive in its inspiration. Extraordinarily, in March, he took out his *First Piano Concerto* and considered revising it for a possible performance in Guildford (this never took place). Putting that score firmly back on the shelf, he reapplied himself to Heath's organ work, writing the second movement (*Interlude*) in July and describing it as "solemnity in excelsis"! The next month he wrote: "organ struggle in sight of its end. Mental dawdling for so long!" He completed the work, then called *Sonata in Division*, on 2 September. Whilst copying it a week later he described it as a "strange Sonata for organ which may become a *Partita*", as indeed it did. On the twenty-eighth he gave the Prime Minister his promised copy whilst Heath was attending the Royal College of Organists' dinner at the Savoy.

The other major keyboard work of this time also had close personal connections, as it was a piano *Sonatina* for Hilary Macnamara. This wonderful late flowering is a tour-de-force of piano writing. Its arguments are compellingly cogent and the writing is nowhere bedevilled by the note-spinning which so often weakened Howells's piano works. Here, the writing in the first movement is energetic, bubbling with exuberance, and almost classical in its economy. The second movement is a particularly fine example of a Howells Saraband. He marks it "Quasi adagio, serioso ma teneramente". Serious it may be, but the thrust is of warmth; a real, communicating and heart-felt warmth. The Finale is a recycling of an earlier Toccata from as long ago as Easter Sunday 1921 and written on that occasion "for Sheanna on the occasion of her marriage: This Toccatissimal proof, if proof were needed that 2 can live as 1". For the *Sonatina*, Howells considerably revised and lengthened the piece which in its first version concerned itself simply with the opening idea.

On 24 January 1972 Hilary Macnamara gave the premiere of the *Sonatina* at the Wigmore Hall ("Hilary's decisive recital"), and soon afterwards, on 23 February, Howells was at the Royal Festival Hall for the premiere of the organ *Partita* given by John Birch, organist of Temple Church, who had advised him about matters of registration prior to publication. Edward Heath was present and wrote warmly to Howells after the event.

Some old friends from Gloucester called Frith used to accommodate Howells regularly when he visited the city. This became a warm relationship over the years, cemented further by a mutual friendship with the Gloucester poet F.W. Harvey, who had written the poem of *Sing Lullaby*. The Harveys were renowned for their hospitality, and the young Howells (and Gurney, too) was a regular visitor to the house called 'Redlands' in Minsterworth. In 1970, after Heath had become Prime Minister, Brian Frith wrote to him, not realising that Howells and Heath were old friends. He suggested Howells for a knighthood. (Howells did not actually want one, saying that "any common or garden industrialist can have one of those!") In the event, the honour which Howells was asked to accept was much more exclusive than a knighthood and he was delighted to be created a Companion of Honour in the Queen's Birthday Honours. He went to Buckingham Palace on 14 June to receive the award from the Queen and talked to her for half an hour.

His eightieth birthday celebrations began in earnest on 7 September when a number of his works were performed and recorded at St John's, Smith Square, including *A Maid Peerless*, the *String Concerto* and the *Elegy*. Hilary Macnamara played the *Piano Sonatina*. The next day Howells himself was the pianist when he went to the BBC's Maida Vale studios to record *Lambert's Clavichord* from which he emerged "... feeling like a professional and public pianist!" On his birthday, 17 October, there was a concert of his music and a reception at the RCM, and a broadcast recital of his choral and organ music from King's College Cambridge.

Sir Adrian Boult (who did not turn down his knighthood) made some highly significant recordings of several of Howells's orchestral works; the *Concerto for Strings* (for EMI), and *Music for a Prince*, the string *Elegy* and *Merry Eye* (for Lyrita Recorded Edition). These were landmark recordings, especially since Howells's orchestral music was completely unknown by this time. With the addition of Boult's recording of his *Procession* on a Lyrita record of Marches, Howells was beginning to be represented, in however small a way, as an orchestral composer. Another landmark recording took place in 1974 when Bernard Richards's chamber ensemble recorded three of Howells's great chamber works; the *Piano Quartet*, the *Fantasy String Quartet* and the *Clarinet Quintet* (with Thea King, Frederick Thurston's widow). All these, together with the outstanding recording made by David Willcocks of *Hymnus Paradisi* with the Bach Choir, and the recording of church music (including the *Collegium Regale* music) he made with the choir of King's College Cambridge, meant that some degree of appraisal was then possible, even in the 1970s, as people came to realise what a substantial composer Howells was in a wide variety of genres.

Work at the RCM continued without any thought of retirement despite his advancing years. It was, of course, a social centre for him, and the students surrounding him helped to keep him young in spirit. There were days when he felt bored to death by the grind of it all, and in one diary entry he articulates his frustration: "the usual day of drudgery at the usual place of endurance"! Drudgery or not, composition work continued unabated, as did his nurturing of friendships all over the country. His music, not to mention his work as an examiner and adjudicator in past years, brought him many new friends and acquaintances. Like many people of his time, Howells was a great letter writer, and a performance of a new work (*Exultate Deo*), commissioned by Lincoln Cathedral for the installation of a new bishop in 1975, led him to write some wonderfully colourful letters to Philip Marshall, the cathedral organist, with whom he formed a very good friendship. Marshall, in return, became a remarkable HH mimic. One letter from Howells dated Shrove Tuesday 1975 is especially revealing. "And here, last evening, pancakes galore! When I was six I would lie awake for the coming of Good Friday: excited; not about Bethlehem, but waiting for the first cry of 'Hot-Cross-Buns!' Ten years old – and a choirboy in Lydney Parish Church – I dreaded a certain 3 hours, and the wretched organ-playing of a tinplate worker at the local mill (which itself, at night, was a vast teeming Hell-flames affair, only a furlong or two from the lovely 13th century church." He then thanks Marshall for the performance, and for sending additional copies (written out in Marshall's own exceptional calligraphic hand, more beautiful even than Herbert's), and goes on: "I loved hearing about a statement by the choirboy about linked arches and phrases. He'll one-day be seeing Eternity in a primrose and finding it again as a last word in 'Jesu, lover of my soul'. (Isn't 'eternity' the very devil of a word to set: even worse than the 'found dead' ('confounded') verdict at the end of 'Te Deum'?)".

On 27 March 1975 Arthur Bliss died peacefully at his home in St John's Wood, London. It was a sad moment for Howells who had shared a lifetime of friendship with Bliss since their student days together at the RCM. Worse, though, was to come all too quickly, for Dorothy suddenly fell ill. Howells was "troubled about D. Very

alarmed at Breakfast. Dr B came to see her – helplessly" Thursday 8
May). She then remained in bed, and for the week of the nineteenth
Howells felt "anxiety for D, acute, most of this week". Then on 26
May: "D's state was giving signs of a decline", and the next day she
was removed to the New Charing Cross Hospital. A brief moment
of happy respite occurred on 7 June, the day when Hilary
Macnamara married the pianist Howard Shelley at St Paul's
Knightsbridge. Herbert then went straight back to Dorothy's bed-
side. In the last few days she had suffered a series of strokes and
things were going from bad to worse: "all this week – U's (Ursula's)
bravery; and comfort for poor D... and for one another!" On 21 June
Dorothy developed pneumonia and was frequently unconscious.
She died the next day. Howells wrote that it was "infinite relief that
she was at rest after her incredible suffering".

There was a great deal of guilty conscience in Howells's final
solicitude to Dorothy as Ursula remembers. "When she was dying,
Herbert used to go three times a day. He used to teach, and in the
lunch hour he would go down to Charing Cross Hospital. When her
brain went, she turned against him. He knew why, and he'd asked
for it. I think he felt only relief when she died, as indeed I did,
because when you get like that, it's all you can pray for, isn't it?"
(UH/PS).

Dorothy was cremated at Putney Vale Crematorium and the
service was "finely" taken by Neil Howells. George Thalben-Ball
played the organ "as he had done in 1920 at our wedding. Many
close friends were there. And a serene day for a serene end of journey". On 27 July, Howells, Ursula and Anthony (her second husband whom she married in 1968) drove to Twigworth to see the
vicar about interring Dorothy's ashes in the plot in which Michael
was buried. On 4 August they "collected the precious dust... and
came home with it. Strange and moving". The next day they
returned to Twigworth "with the urn for D's burial there".

After this, Howells showed signs of increasing loneliness.
Although he was still going into the RCM quite regularly, his written
thoughts become more reflective of past times, and references to
loneliness appear again and again: "a day alone: seemingly endless".
He was still composing however, and motets were still pouring from

him. These included *Come, My Soul* written in September 1972 for his friend Richard Latham (organist of St Paul's, Knightsbridge and an RCM colleague); and two complex and challenging motets for David Willcocks on texts by George Herbert, *Sweetest of Sweets* and *Antiphon*. Howells first heard these three pieces "inadequately sung" by the three cathedral choirs in Pershore Abbey as part of the Worcester Three Choirs Festival in 1978. He had certainly not lost his critical faculties. Other motets were written: *I would be true* for the wedding of Lionel and Elisabeth Dakers's daughter Rachel (Lionel Dakers was currently Director of the Royal School of Church Music); *The fear of the Lord* for John Rutter's choir at Clare College Cambridge. Howells also completed one last set of canticles for Dallas, USA.

Having finished writing the setting of Herbert's *Antiphon* in April 1977, and following yet another highly successful performance of *Hymnus Paradisi* at Gloucester conducted in August by Donald Hunt (organist of Worcester Cathedral), Howells attended the "induction of the Vicar of Bray" on 10 October. His nephew Neil, of whom he was so fond, always took the family funerals, and Howells said of him: "he'll bury the lot of us before he's finished". It was sadly, if not surprisingly, to be proved true. However, Howells's comment on this occasion was simply that he was tickled pink that his nephew and Godson had been appointed Vicar of Bray: "the best-known appointment in the Church of England after the Archbishop of Canterbury!" (NH/PS).

On 8 December 1977 Lord Blake, Master of The Queen's College Oxford, wrote to offer Howells an Honorary Fellowship of the College which he was pleased to accept. Sadly, he never managed to attend any functions because of his gradually deteriorating condition. It was a singular honour in recognition of a man who had been a (non-resident) member of the College in order to sit his B. Mus and D. Mus examinations.

On 17 September 1978 (Ursula's birthday) Howells had a very serious fall at home. Trying, as usual, to rush around despite his advancing years, he tumbled to the bottom of the stairs seriously injuring his left hand. So serious was it, in fact, that he was discovered with all his fingers smashed and the bone sticking through flesh. The surgeon thought he might never recover the use of it, but he reckoned without Howells's gritty determination in the face of a huge personal challenge. Howells went on to effect an extraordinary recovery despite his great age.

Howells's last day of teaching at the Royal College of Music, 12 July 1979, was a momentous day for him. He attended the Prize-Giving at the College at 3 p.m. followed by Afternoon Tea, and in the evening attended a College performance of Mozart's *Magic Flute*. He wrote: "Thursday 12th concluded my 59 years on the teaching staff of the RCM". No other musician alive or dead could make such a claim. Given far more stringent retirement regulations these days, it is unlikely that anyone will again. It is a remarkable record of loyalty and devotion to a single institution. Despite the great love-hate relationship he had with it over the years, it was still the haunt of so many benign ghosts, Parry and Stanford chief amongst them. To that extent he would have counted it disloyal to these great and revered men to leave 'their' institution before his time was really up.

In 1980 he had another bad fall in January and Ursula had to come post-haste from her home in Brighton to deal with the situation. In June Herbert went to Tewkesbury Abbey to hear *Hymnus Paradisi* live for the last time, returning to Gloucestershire for one final visit in August, and coming back via Vaughan Williams's birthplace at Down Ampney, "an amazing moment". Valerie Trimble died on 16 November "a mercy ending to cruelty ended" and was cremated at Putney Vale on the twenty-first. After this, Howells began a slow decline to the end. Diary entries are few for the rest of 1980, and his last diary, that for 1981, is ragged, untidy, and with only sporadic entries. He made one very endearing slip for the entry on his daughter's birthday on 17 September, when he wrote: "Beloved Ursulove's birthday".

There was one final important ceremony related to the Royal College of Music which he had to attend in 1980, when he was awarded an honorary Doctorate of the College. The Queen Mother, being President, made awards to Howells and to Boult, who was being similarly honoured, on the same day. The ceremony took place at Clarence House, but Boult being more frail than Howells at this stage (they were the same age), had to receive his sitting in his car "whilst the Queen Mother stood in a puddle" (as Ursula Howells, who was escorting her father, remembers with wry amusement). Howells went up steps to the Drawing Room to receive his framed citation and became rather confused as to who was giving what to whom. At one point he thought he might be supposed to be making a presentation to the Queen Mother. Howells who, at this stage, was only safe drinking a small sherry, when asked by the Queen Mother what he would like to drink, asked for white wine. Correctly interpreting an intervention by Ursula, ("is that wise, darling?"), the Queen Mother safely delivered the required sherry and all was well.

The last great public occasion Howells attended was the Gala Concert at the Royal Festival Hall in honour of his ninetieth birthday on the day itself, 17 October 1982. Once again it was Sir David Willcocks who made the great gesture to an old friend in bringing to life once more the *Missa Sabrinensis*, which had barely seen the light of day since his Festival at Worcester in 1954. It was a great occasion, and Howells, frail as he was, stood to wave in acknowledgement of the applause from a grateful audience.

The last period of Howells's life was sad, and was impossibly difficult for his daughter who, at the same time as nursing her father, was also having to nurse her husband, Anthony, who had had a serious stroke which left him physically disabled and without speech. She tells the story of her father's final decline:

As his brain began to fail Herbert couldn't accept the fact that Anthony had had a stroke, and it got to the stage when he wouldn't let anyone come into the house to look after him so that Anthony and I could have a break. He would say 'You go. I'm perfectly all right on my own'. He had flooded the house twice, and almost set fire to it. I couldn't. Finally, I was so tired trying to cope with both... that the doctor tried to persuade Herbert to go into a home for a fortnight so we could have a holiday. That didn't work as, despite agreeing to his face, the moment the doctor's back was turned, Herbert insisted that he would be perfectly all right by himself at home. Finally, I had to be tough and I took him to this very nice nursing home in Putney. I said to him 'it's for two weeks'. By this time he was incontinent. I was having to lift him all the time. I felt terrible because he knew; he just knew he wouldn't come out. He sat with his head in his hands. He wouldn't speak, he wouldn't do anything. And the sister said I was just to go and that she would ring if it was absolutely necessary. I had been in Brighton in the flat for about four days when they rang to say that he had had another slight stroke. Finally, I came back early, because I was worried, and he didn't know me. He died two days later.

It's a well-known thing that if you put people in an environment where they feel alien, they will last about six weeks. He did not want to die, and he was furious. By the end he was semi-conscious, so he didn't know. He never realised how old he was, and he never made any allowances for age. He was a remarkable man and a loving and understanding father.

In the last months I saw that 'Hymnus' was on the radio and I told him it was on. He asked what it was. I told him that he had written it for Michael. He said 'I don't want to hear it', but I just left it on. And I went through at the end of it, and there he was just lying there with tears streaming down his face saying 'did I write that?'

(UH/PS)

Herbert Howells died on 23 February 1983 aged ninety (Elgar had also died on 23 February in 1934). His great friend and colleague Sir Adrian Boult had died the night before. Howells's funeral took place, as had his wife's before him, at Putney Vale Crematorium. Once again, Neil Howells officiated and Thalben-Ball, now ninety-one years old, played the organ. Sir David Willcocks warned Neil Howells that Thalben-Ball was a little erratic at that stage, but that if there was any sign of a problem he would take over. Thalben-Ball asked when he should play at the end of the service. Neil Howells told him that he would speak the words of "Holy is the true light", the words of the last movement of *Hymnus Paradisi*, and would then give him a 'knowing look'. Neil remarked that he would never forget Thalben-Ball's beaming eyes as he began to play the *Chosen Tune* which Howells had written for his wedding in 1920 (NH/PS).

On 3 June there was a Service of Thanksgiving for Howells's life in Westminster Abbey during which his ashes were interred in the north aisle. Sir Thomas Armstrong read the lesson, Sir David

Willcocks gave the address, and Neil Howells took the prayer of commendation. The choir sang *Take him, earth for cherishing*, *Like as the Hart* and the *Collegium Regale Te Deum*. Hymns were sung to tunes by Howells (his *Michael* tune), Vaughan Williams and Parry. Howells then joined the great musicians of his time including Elgar, Vaughan Williams, Stanford, Walton and Boult in a roll call of all those who helped this country build its own identity as a musical nation.

Howells lived a very long life during the course of which the whole world changed. He watched those changes, developing and growing through them, but taking only those as influences which he felt continued to contribute beauty to the world. As such, whilst he was entirely aware of new trends in music and the arts, he was not materially affected by the experiments going on all around him. His was, to that extent, a cul-de-sac of lovely things. In a BBC programme towards the end of his life he said: "I have composed out of sheer love of trying to make nice sounds. I have written really, to put it simply, the music I would like to write and for no other reason. I love music as a man can love a woman. The one thing now which keeps me alive and makes me want to be alive is just that I love music" (BBC/Prizeman). This makes him no less meaningful in the overall scheme of things. Hugh Ottaway described perfectly the essence of Howells's magic in an article he wrote about *Hymnus Paradisi*. It is as fitting a conclusion to this story as any: "The strength of the music derives from its impeccable style, from the mode and quality of thought within the idiom. That's what tells in any work of art. Idioms come and go and history finds little to choose between them; the enduring factor is the quality of thought, which alone makes the idiom a living and vital thing" (MO 1951).

Series Afterword

The Border country is that region between England and Wales which is upland and lowland, both and neither. Centuries ago kings and barons fought over these Marches without their national allegiance ever being settled. It is beautiful, gentle, intriguing, and often surprising. It displays majestic landscapes, which show a lot, and hide some more. People now walk it, poke into its cathedrals and bookshops, and fly over or hang-glide from its mountains, yet its mystery remains.

The subjects covered in the present series seem united by a particular kind of vision. Writers as diverse as Mary Webb, Dennis Potter and Thomas Traherne, painters and composers such as David Jones and Edward Elgar, and writers on the Welsh side such as Henry Vaughan and Arthur Machen, bear one imprint of the border woods, rivers, villages and hills. This vision is set in a special light, a cloudy, golden twilight so characteristic of the region. As you approach the border you feel it. Suddenly you are in that finally elusive terrain, looking from a bare height down on to a plain, or from the lower land up to a gap in the hills, and you want to explore it, maybe not to return.

There are more earthly aspects. From England the border meant romantic escape or colonial appropriation; from Wales it was roads to London, education or employment. Boundaries are necessarily political. Much is shared, yet different languages are spoken, in more than one sense. The series authors reflect the diversity of their subjects. They are specialists or academics; critics or biographers; poets or musicians themselves; or ordinary people with however an established reputation of writing imaginatively and directly about what moves them. They are of various ages, both sexes, Welsh and English, border people themselves or from further afield.

A former pupil of the composer, Paul Spicer underlines that Herbert Howells remade church music for this century. Probably not a day goes by without one of his services or anthems being sung in a cathedral or church somewhere in Britain and this is likely to continue. Yet his inspiration came as much from secular things as from sacred: his thirty-odd years in London; his wayward private life; and the tragic deaths: of John F. Kennedy, and of his own nine-year-old son; both in their wholly different impacts led to outstanding works. On a different front: Howells leads a curious trend in English sacred music in that so many of its chief composers of our time have come from or spent many years in the England-Wales border country. Ralph Vaugan Williams, Edward Elgar, Hubert Parry, Samuel Sebastian Wesley, Gerald Finzi, Peter Warlock, E.J. Moeran, and Herbert Howells himself. In combing specialist interpretation of the music with a moving human account of the life, Paul Spicer's study enables us to decide on this and other questions for the first time. It is an unprecedented work.

John Powell Ward

Bibliography

The abbreviated codes used in the text to refer to sources are given in brackets. The following codes refer to magazines: CSM: *Christian Science Monitor*; MT: *Musicial Times*; M&L: *Music and Letters*.

Books

Stephen Banfield *Gerald Finzi: An English Composer* (London: Faber, 1997) (GF)

Stephen Banfield *Sensibility and English Song* (Cambridge: CUP, 1985) (SES)

Anthony Boden *Three Choirs: A History of the Festival* (Stroud: Alan Sutton, 1992)

J. Charles Cox *The Little Guides: Gloucestershire* (London: Methuen, 1914)

Oliver Davies & Fiona Bowie *Celtic Christian Spirituality (An Anthology of Medieval and Modern Sources)* (London: SPCK, 1995, 1997)

Lewis Foreman *From Parry to Britten: British Music in Letters 1900-1945* (London: Batsford, 1987) (LF)

Peter Hodgson D.Phil Thesis University of Colorado, 1970 (PH)

Frank Howes *The English Musical Renaissance* (London: Secker & Warburg, 1966) (FH)

Michael Hurd *The Ordeal of Ivor Gurney* (Oxford: OUP, 1978) (MH)

Arthur Mee *The King's England: Gloucestershire* (London: Hodder & Stoughton. 1938, 1940, 1947)

Christopher Palmer *Herbert Howells A Celebration* (London: Thames, 1992, 1996) (CPC)

Christopher Palmer *Herbert Howells A Study* (London: Novello, 1978) (CPS)

BIBLIOGRAPHY

Russell Palmer *British Music* (London: Skelton Robinson, 1947) (BM)

Alan Ridout *A Composer's Life* (London: Thames, 1995) (AR)

Robert Spearing *HH: A tribute to Herbert Howells on his 80th birthday* (London: Triad Press, 1972)

Robert Spearing RCM GRSM dissertation on Howells (RS/RCM)

Helen Waddell *Songs of the Wandering Scholars* (London: Folio Society, 1982) (SWS)

Articles from periodicals

Felix Aprahamian 'The Kent Yeoman' *Musical Times* Nov 1953

B.W.G.R. Reviews of Music: 'Missa Sabrinensis' *Music and Letters* Jan 1955

Katherine Eggar 'An English Composer: Herbert Howells' *The Music Teacher* Dec 1923 (TMT)

Edwin Evans 'Modern British Composers VIII: Herbert Howells' *Musical Times* Feb 1920

Gerald Finzi 'Herbert Howells' *Musical Times* April 1954

Scott Goddard Review of 'Missa Sabrinensis' *Musical Times* Nov 1954

Harvey Grace 'Herbert Howells's Organ Sonata' *Musical Times* April 1934

Sydney Grew 'Herbert Howells: his "In Gloucestershire"' *Christian Science Monitor* 15.12.20

Herbert Howells 'Vaughan Williams's Pastoral Symphony' *Music and Letters* April 1922

Herbert Howells article on Charles Wood published by the RSCM 1966 (ECM 1966)

Frank Howes 'Howells and the Anglican Tradition' *English Church Music* 1969 (ECM)

A. Eaglefield Hull 'The A Capella Music of Herbert Howells' *Musical Opinion* Feb 1920 (MO)

Reginald Jaques 'Howells's *Hymnus Paradisi*' *Music and Letters* July 1952

G.M. Review of 'Stabat Mater' *Musical Opinion* Jan 1963

Colin Mason Review of Howells's 'Clarinet Sonata' *Musical Times* Jan 1956

Arthur Milner 'The Organ Sonata of Herbert Howells' *Musical Times* Dec 1964

Hugh Ottaway: '*Hymnus Paradisi*: an appreciation' *Musical Opinion* 1951 (MO 1951)

Marion Scott 'Herbert Howells' *The Music Student* Nov 1918 (TMS)

Marion Scott 'Folk-Song Gift to Herbert Howells' *Christian Science Monitor* 11.9.20.

Marion Scott 'Introduction: Herbert Howells' *The Music Bulletin* Vol VI May 1924

Unattributed 'A Young Composer of Promise' *Christian Science Monitor* 14.6.19

John Weeks 'Howells's Salisbury Period' *Musical Times* April 1986

Substantial Reviews in National Papers

Rachel Trickett Review of 'A Tribute to Walter de la Mare' *Daily Telegraph* 1968

Unattributed 'A Distinguished Composer for the Anglican Liturgy: Church Music of Herbert Howells' *The Times* 25 May 1956

Interviews and other sources

Sleeve note for Argo ZRG507 by Herbert Howells (with permission of the Decca Recording Company) (Argo)

Booklet note on Howells's *Mass in the Dorian Mode* by Patrick Russill for Chandos CHAN9021 (Chandos)

Talk for BBC Third Programme by Herbert Howells on 15.11.40. (BBC November 1940)

Discussion between Herbert Howells and Sir Arthur Bliss recorded for an interval talk on BBC Radio 3 in 1972 (BBC 1972)

'Echoes of a Lifetime' BBC Radio 3, compiled and presented by Robert Prizeman 1981 (BBC/Prizeman)

'Out of the Deep' BBC Radio 3, compiled and presented by Andrew Green 1992 (BBC/Green)

Interview between Eric Smith and Paul Spicer (ES/PS)

BIBLIOGRAPHY

Interview between Sir John Margetson and Paul Spicer (JM/PS)
Interview between John Williams and Paul Spicer (JW/PS)
Interviews between Ursula Howells and Paul Spicer (UH/PS)
Correspondence between Sir John Margetson and Christopher Robinson (JM/CR)

Acknowledgements

My first exposure to Howells's music was as a chorister at New College, Oxford. It was there I 'caught the bug' which has led, some thirty-five years later, to the writing of this book. I would like to thank my parents for sending me there, despite the problems encountered on that particular journey, and Sir David Lumsden for introducing me to this sound-world at such an impressionable age.

In a book such as this, written about someone who died so comparatively recently, it is inevitable that there were many people whom I had the good fortune to meet and to talk to who knew Herbert Howells personally. When I knew him, it was as one of his composition students at the Royal College of Music in the early 1970s when he was coming into his eighties. Whilst he was certainly an old man, he had lost nothing of his old sparkle, as friend and fellow student Robert Spearing will testify. Whilst I was keen to get him talking as much as possible about his generation, his times and his teachers, Robert was much more probing, and much more aware of the importance of writing everything down as it happened or was said. He wrote the very first monograph about HH. I have been much indebted to him and grateful for access to his researches and notes made at that important time, including the opportunity of hearing his wonderfully atmospheric tape of Howells having Afternoon Tea (Howells's capitals) at Robert's flat with the artist Richard Walker. Hearing just how much Herbert loved tea, toast and jam, brought home what a sensualist he was, even at this level. Like many others I have had the good fortune to talk to, Robert has been a source of constant encouragement to me throughout.

None, however, has been more generous in every way than Ursula Howells. I am so grateful to her for her kindness, and for the objective way in which she was able to discuss deeply personal matters, helping me to be able to write about them with greater confidence in 'telling it straight'. Her sparkle and candour make her singular; but her deep feelings for her father, mother and brother (the latter so central in this story), put a special responsibility on a biographer in so personal a tale as this. It is hoped that what has preceded is fair in all the limited scope of its brief, as it is told with love and respect.

It has also been a great pleasure to meet and talk to others in the Howells family who had fascinating stories to tell. In particular, I would like to thank Joyce Garnett (daughter of Howells's brother Richard) for her hospitality, and for trusting me with valuable family photographs, an original Howells song manuscript from 1914 (previously unknown), and other family documents. On the same occasion I also had the pleasure of meeting the Rev. Neil Howells (Leslie's son) and his wife Olive. Neil also provided me with much valuable personal information.

Others who have given freely of their time and help are the late Alan Ridout, Sir Edward Heath, Sir David Willcocks, John Williams, Sir John Margetson, the Rev. John O'Brian (vicar of Twigworth), Eric Smith, Charles Carson, Lydney Library, Lydney Archive Shop, the librarians at the Royal College of Music (in particular Peter Horton), Melville Watts, Peter Howells (son of Herbert's brother Howard), Michael Darke (who kindly supplied me with the letters from Herbert to his father), Brian Frith, Jean Finzi, Andrew Green, Andrew Millinger, and Justin Sillman who has given me such frequent and invaluable help with the mysteries of my computer. I have also been much indebted to Paul Andrews for his index of Howells's works in Christopher Palmer's *Centenary Celebration*.

Special thanks are reserved for two individuals without whom this book could never have been written. First; Christopher Palmer, upon whose comprehensive researches into all aspects of Howells's life and work I have drawn freely. I make no apologies for this. Christopher was a master in many fields and gave new vigour to them all. Everyone who loves the music of Herbert Howells owes him an enormous debt of gratitude. I enjoyed many hours in his company discussing Howells, and he was very helpful to me in the preparation of the *Sine Nomine* score for performance at Gloucester in 1992. I hope that this book will not only compliment his fascinating *Centenary Celebration* by telling the story of Howells's life as a chronological tale, but that it will also act as my personal, if wholly inadequate, tribute to Christopher's memory.

The last person to thank is also, in some senses the first, as it was through him that this book came to be written. John Powell Ward, the series editor of Border Lines, asked me to write about Howells back in the Autumn of 1994. He has been a source of sympathetic encouragement throughout the long periods of inactivity when other projects had to take precedence, as well as in these more recent times of solid work. It was his belief in my ability to tell this heartfelt story which made it a reality.

Paul Spicer
Lichfield
January 1998

Index

INDEX

Royal Choral Society, 148
Royal College of Art, 116
Royal College of Music, 23, 24, 25,
    28, 31, 32, 33, 34, 37, 39, 44, 49, 52,
    54, 55, 63, 69, 72, 74, 77, 80, 85, 87,
    91, 95, 105, 107, 114, 119, 120, 123,
    124, 125, 127, 128, 151, 156, 174,
    175, 178, 179, 180, 181, 182
    Howells's Room 19, 129
Royal College of Organists, 33, 43,
    168, 177
Royal Festival Hall, 150, 156, 177,
    183
Royal Philharmonic Orchestra, 113
Royal Philharmonic Society, 80
Royal School of Church Music, 181

Salisbury Cathedral, 49, 50, 51, 52,
    54, 55, 56, 61, 62, 122, 126, 134,
    144
Sammons, Alfred, 60
Samuel, Harold, 80
Sandwich, Earl of, 71, 150
Sargent, Sir Malcolm, 80, 144, 156
Scholes, Percy, 80
Scott, Marion, 14, 45, 46, 53, 71, 73,
    157
Sheffield Cathedral, 25
Shelley, Howard, 180
Shimmin, Sydney, 82
Smale, Kathleen, 28, 84
Southwark Cathedral, 157
Spearing, Robert, 87, 103
Spencer Dyke String Quartet, 77
St Alban's Cathedral, 138
    Acoustics, 138
St John's, Smith Square, 111, 178
St Mary Redcliffe, Bristol, 15
St Michael's, Cornhill, 50, 150, 164
St Michael's Singers, 50, 164
St Paul's Girls' School, 103, 105, 106,
    114, 119, 127
St Paul's, Kinghtsbridge, 180, 181
St Peter's Basilica, Rome, 169
Stafford, Hubert, 25

Stanford, Guy (Charles Stanford's
    son), 152
Stanford, Sir Charles, 23, 24, 25, 31,
    32, 34, 35, 36, 37, 43, 47, 48, 49, 51,
    60, 61, 67, 74, 79, 131, 152, 169,
    182, 185
    Signet ring, 47, 152, 168
    Beati Quorum Via, 135
    Evening Canticles in A, 131
    Evening Canticles in C, 131
    Evening Canticles in G, 131
    Stabat Mater, 169
    The Travelling Companion, 48
Stevenson, Robert Louis, 21
Stravinsky, Igor, 39
Sumsion, Herbert, 43, 99, 116, 124,
    144, 145, 146

Tallis, Thomas, 22, 36
Tear, Robert, 172
Terry, Sir R.R., 35, 36, 57, 61, 74, 88,
    89
Tewkesbury Abbey, 182
Thalben-Ball, Sir George, 71, 74, 90,
    151, 180, 184
The Athenaeum, 55
Three Choirs Festival, 17, 18, 22, 57,
    74, 157
    Gloucester, 17, 18, 22, 23, 39, 75,
        100, 107, 144, 145, 146, 167,
        181, 183
    Hereford, 146, 152, 176
    Worcester, 18, 146, 148, 156, 159,
        181
Thurston, Frederick, 32, 157, 178
Tippett, Sir Michael, 154, 156
Trimble, Valerie, 94, 106, 182
Twigworth, Glos, 45, 72, 98, 99, 103,
    105

Vatican Motu Proprio 1903, 36
Vaughan Williams, Ralph, 13, 20, 22,
    23, 24, 26, 27, 36, 48, 49, 59, 75, 78,
    80, 86, 89, 90, 103, 115, 116, 130,
    144, 146, 152, 153, 154, 156, 168,

Author Note

Paul Spicer, a former student of Howells, is the founder and director of the Finzi Singers; Professor of Choral Conducting at the Royal College of Music; and conductor of the Birmingham Bach Choir. He is Artistic Director of the Lichfield Festival and is much in demand as a composer, recording producer and broadcaster. A lifelong advocate of Howells's music, he has published articles, created programmes for BBC Radio 3 (including a 'Composer of the Week' series), and recorded much of his choral music.

The Border Lines Series

Elizabeth Barrett Browning Barbara Dennis

Bruce Chatwin Nicholas Murray

The Dymock Poets Sean Street

Edward Elgar: Sacred Music John Allison

Margiad Evans: Ceridwen Lloyd-Morgan

Eric Gill & David Jones at Capel-y-Ffin Jonathan Miles

Gerard Manley Hopkins in Wales Norman White

A.E. Housman Keith Jebb

Francis Kilvert David Lockwood

Arthur Machen Mark Valentine

Wilfred Owen Merryn Williams

Edith Pargeter: Ellis Peters Margaret Lewis

Dennis Potter Peter Stead

John Cowper Powys Herbert Williams

Philip Wilson Steer Ysanne Holt

Henry Vaughan Stevie Davies

Mary Webb Gladys Mary Coles

Samuel Sebastian Wesley Donald Hunt

Raymond Williams Tony Pinkney

Francis Brett Young Michael Hall